HENRY GEORGE

Jacob Oser, Ph.D.
Professor of Economics
Utica College of Syracuse University

SERIES EDITORS

Arthur W. Brown, Ph.D.
Professor of English and
Dean of the School of Liberal
Arts and Sciences, Baruch College; and

Thomas S. Knight, Ph. D.
Professor and Chairman of the
Department of Philosophy, Adelphi University

Twayne Publishers, Inc.   ::   New York

Copyright © 1974 by Twayne Publishers, Inc.

Library of Congress Cataloging in Publication Data

Oser, Jacob, 1915-
  Henry George.

  (Great thinkers series)
  Bibliography: p.
  1. George, Henry, 1839-1897. 2. George, Henry,
1839-1897. Progress and poverty.
HB119.G4083   330'.092'4 [B]   73-13895
  ISBN 0-8057-3682-4

MANUFACTURED IN THE UNITED STATES OF AMERICA

To those who are still struggling
for a better world

Contents

	PAGE
Chronology	9
1. THE LIFE OF HENRY GEORGE BEFORE *PROGRESS AND POVERTY*	17
Childhood in Philadelphia	17
The Youth at Sea	19
The Young Man in California	21
George Becomes a Writer	23
The Birth of Progress and Poverty	27
2. A GUIDE TO *PROGRESS AND POVERTY*	32
Book I. *Wages and Capital*	33
Book II. *Population and Subsistence*	35
Book III. *The Laws of Distribution*	38
Book IV. *Effect of Material Progess Upon the Distribution of Wealth*	40
Book V. *The Problem Solved*	43
Book VI. *The Remedy*	44
Book VII. *Justice of the Remedy*	46
Book VIII. *Application of the Remedy*	47
Book IX. *Effects of the Remedy*	48
3. EVALUATION OF *PROGRESS AND POVERTY*	51
The Validity of Progress and Poverty	51
Is the Landlords' Share Rising and Labor's Falling?	54
George's Confusion of the Law of Diminishing Returns, Increasing Returns to Scale, and Growing Efficiency	56
The Inadequacy of the "Single Tax"	62
George's Misconceptions About the Nature of Capitalism	63

PAGE

4. THE PUBLIC'S RECEPTION OF HENRY GEORGE
   AND *PROGRESS AND POVERTY*   68

   Public Support for Henry George and Progress and
      Poverty   69
   George's Conflict with Herbert Spencer   73
   The Opposition of Prominent Economists   75
   The Opposition of The New York Times   80
   Socialist Criticisms of George   82

5. OTHER WRITING OF HENRY GEORGE   86

   "The Irish Land Question"   86
   Social Problems   88
   Protection or Free Trade   92
   "An Open Letter to Pope Leo XIII"   96
   The Science of Political Economy   103

6. THE LIFE OF HENRY GEORGE AFTER *PROGRESS
   AND POVERTY*   108

   George's Speaking Tours Abroad   108
   George's Fight Against Poverty—His Own and the World's   112
   George's Two Campaigns for Mayor of New York City   114

SELECTED BIBLIOGRAPHY   121

INDEX   127

Chronology

1839 On September 2 Henry George was born in Philadelphia, second
child and oldest son of Richard and Catherine George.

1853 Henry left high school after five months, which was the last of
his formal education.

1855 In April he sailed on the merchant ship *Hindoo* as foremast boy
on a 14 months trip to Australia and India.

1856 He became an apprentice typesetter in Philadelphia.

1857 In December he left for California on the light-house tender
Shubrick as ship's storekeeper.

1858 Lured by the report of gold discoveries along the Frazer River,
he went to Victoria on Vancouver Island, Canada; he returned to
San Francisco in November "dead broke," and found work as a
typesetter.

1860 As soon as he became twenty-one years old, Henry George
joined the typographical union. Shortly afterward he became a
foreman printer on the *California Home Journal.*

1861 He became a partner in the San Francisco *Daily Evening Journal,*
and withdrew when the partnership was dissolved. He and Annie
Fox were married on December 3. He found work as a substitute
typesetter on the *Union,* a morning daily paper, published in
Sacramento.

1862 On November 3 Henry George, Jr. was born. (He was to be the
first biographer of his father, and he afterward was elected to the
United States House of Representatives from New York.)

1864 George lost his job on the Sacramento *Union* and became a
printer on the San Francisco *Evening Journal* and other papers.
He entered a partnership in a job-printing business.

1865 Richard Fox George, the second child, was born on January 27.
(He was to become a sculptor.) Henry George abandoned the
job-printing business and worked hard at perfecting his writing

skill. He published several articles, including "Sic Semper Tyrannis!" on the death of Lincoln. He was a typesetter and a reporter for the newspaper *Alta California.* Then he became a typesetter on state printing in California.

1866 George became a typesetter for the San Francisco *Times.* His editorials were accepted for publication, and he quickly became a reporter and then an editorial writer for the paper.

1867 He became managing editor of the San Francisco *Times.* The third child, Jennie Teresa George, was born.

1868 He became managing editor of the San Francisco *Chronicle,* and he was later sent to New York City by the San Francisco *Herald. The Overland Monthly* published his article, "What the Railroad Will Bring Us."

1869 He failed in his fight against the monopoly combination of the Associated Press and Western Union. The *New York Tribune* published his article opposing Chinese immigration. George became editor of the Oakland *Daily Transcript,* in which he published a letter from John Stuart Mill commenting on his *Tribune* article on Chinese immigration.

1870 George became editor and part owner of the *Sacramento Reporter.* When the railroad interests bought the paper, he left it.

1871 The Democratic Party nominated George for the state Assembly, but he lost the election. He published a pamphlet, "Our Land and Land Policy, National and State," that was a forerunner of *Progress and Poverty.* He became a partner and editor of the San Francisco *Daily Evening Post,* the first paper west of the Rocky Mountains to sell for a penny a copy.

1872 George was elected as a delegate to the Democratic National Convention in Baltimore, and at the convention he was elected secretary of the California delegation. He supported Horace Greeley for president.

1875 George and his partners lost control over the *Daily Evening Post* because of financial difficulties.

1876 The new Democratic governor of California appointed George State Inspector of Gas Meters because of his political help and to enable him to do some writing. He delivered his first formal speech in support of Samuel J. Tilden, Democratic candidate for president of the United States. He became a leading speaker in California during the campaign.

1877 He lectured at the University of California in Berkeley on "The Study of Political Economy." He was designated "the Orator of the Day" at the Fourth of July celebration in San Francisco. On September 18 he began to write *Progress and Poverty.* On October 2 the fourth and last child, Anna Angela George, was born. (She was to be his second child to write his biography.)

1879 *Progress and Poverty* was published.

1880 George moved to New York City, where he lived for the rest of his life.

1881 George published the pamphlet, "The Irish Land Question," later republished as "The Land Question." He lectured in Canada, and he left for his first lecture tour in the United Kingdom with his wife and daughters in October, 1881.

1882 George was arrested twice in western Ireland. He returned to New York in October.

1883 *Social Problems,* George's second book, was published. He sailed with his older son for a second lecture tour in the United Kingdom.

1884 He returned to New York in April. He went to Canada a second time to speak under the auspices of the Knights of Labor. In October he left for his third speaking tour in the United Kingdom and returned early in the following year.

1886 George's third book, *Protection or Free Trade,* was published. In his first campaign for mayor of New York City he came in second, ahead of Theodore Roosevelt.

1887 George published and edited a new weekly newspaper, *The Standard,* in New York City. He ran for Secretary of State of New York State and lost.

1888 He spent two weeks in the United Kingdom on his fourth trip there.

1889 He returned to the United Kingdom with his wife and daughters on his fifth trip there; he also went to Paris to attend a land reform conference.

1890 He sailed with his wife from San Francisco to lecture in

Australia. On his way back to the United States he stopped in the United Kingdom for the sixth time to deliver some lectures. He returned to the United States in September, where he had his first stroke in December.

1891 George withdrew from *The Standard* in order to devote all his time to writing; this was made possible by the generosity of wealthy friends who supported him financially. He published "An Open Letter to Pope Leo XIII," in answer to the Pope's Encyclical Letter on the Condition of Labor.

1892 George published his fourth book, *A Perplexed Philosopher.*

1896 He visited both the Republican and Democratic national conventions, and he supported William Jennings Bryan for the presidency.

1897 Against medical advice, he ran a second time for mayor of New York City. A stroke killed him on Friday, October 29, four days before the elections.

1898 Henry George's fifth book, *The Science of Political Economy,* though unfinished, was published posthumously.

HENRY GEORGE

CHAPTER 1

The Life of Henry George Before Progress and Poverty

Henry George was a little man (not quite five feet six inches tall) who strode across the stage of world affairs like a giant. A high school dropout, he educated himself and became a powerful thinker, writer, public speaker and organizer. World-famous figures—professors, philosophers, popes, statesmen, preachers, businessmen and writers—listened to him and grappled with his ideas whether they agreed with him or not. Common people flocked to his cause by the millions. He organized triumphant speaking tours in the British Isles, in Canada and in Australia as well as in his native land. He was also an able organizer, as seen by the great reform movement he sparked and led.

Childhood in Philadelphia

Henry George was born in Philadelphia on September 2, 1839. His father, Richard George, was a clerk in the Philadelphia Custom House. He left his position to become a partner in a business that published and sold books for the Protestant Episcopal Church and related Bible and prayer book societies. One of the associates in the business was George S. Appleton, who afterward became one of the owners of a large publishing house which published Henry George's most famous work, *Progress and Poverty*. Richard George's publishing venture failed in the end, and he returned to the Custom House as a clerk.

Henry George's mother was Catherine Pratt Vallance. She received a good boarding school education, and she and her sister were operating a small private school when she left to marry Richard George. They had six daughters and four sons. Henry was their second child and the oldest boy.

By the time Henry George entered high school, he was acutely aware of the difficulty his parents had in raising a large family on wages of $800 a year. Besides, the lad grew impatient with formal education. He was known for quickness of thought, originality and general information. Years later Henry George said that at high school he was "for the most part idle and wasted time." He felt that he should be supporting himself instead of being a financial burden on his parents. After less than five months in high school, Henry received his father's permission to leave school and go to work. He was then not quite 14 years old, and he never received any formal education after that. But his fondness for reading, his keen mind and his sharply observant eyes enabled him to educate himself with remarkable results.

In a lecture delivered at the University of California in 1877, George showed the results of this education in a story of how he reasoned why an iron ship floated:

When I was a boy I went down to the wharf with another boy to see the first iron steamship which had ever crossed the ocean to our port. Now, hearing of an iron steamship seemed to us then a good deal like hearing of a leaden kite or a wooden cooking stove. But, we had not been long aboard of her, before my companion said in a tone of contemptuous disgust: "Pooh! I see how it is. She's all lined with wood; that's the reason she floats." I could not controvert him for the moment, but I was not satisfied, and sitting down on the wharf when he left me, I set to work trying mental experiments. If it was the wood inside of her that made her float, then the more wood the higher she would float; and mentally I loaded her up with wood. But, as I was familiar with the process of making boats out of blocks of wood, I at once saw that, instead of floating higher, she would sink deeper. Then I mentally took all the wood out of her, as we dug out our wooden boats, and saw that thus lightened she would float higher still. Then, in imagination, I jammed a hole in her, and saw that the water would run in and she would sink, as did our wooden boats when ballasted with leaden keels. And thus I saw, as clearly as though I could have actually made these experiments with the steamer, that it was not the wooden lining that made her float, but her hollowness, or as I would now phrase it, her displacement of water.[1]

1. Henry George, Jr., *The Life of Henry George* (New York: Robert Schalkenbach Foundation, 1960), p. 13. [Originally published in 1900.]

Young Henry's first job was wrapping packages and running errands for a china and glass shop at two dollars a week. Later he was a clerk in the office of a marine adjuster. This restless youth went to sea and had sailed to Australia and India by the time he was 17.

The Youth at Sea

In 1855 Henry signed up as foremast boy for six dollars a month on the merchant sailing ship *Hindoo,* bound for Australia and India on a voyage that lasted fourteen months. The crew went on strike in Melbourne; they were rebelling against the harsh conditions that were so typical on ships, and they had caught the "gold fever," hoping to strike gold as prospectors. The crew was sentenced to a month's hard labor and a new crew was signed on to complete the voyage.

Though the captain of the *Hindoo* was Henry's benefactor and a friend of the George family, Henry's sympathies were with the striking sailors. Although he did not go on strike himself, years later he defended effectively the rights of seamen. In 1873 the ship *Sunrise* sailed from New York to San Francisco. The captain was brutal enough toward the men that three of them, who had been kidnapped on to the ship in the first place, jumped overboard and were drowned. Word of these conditions got around San Francisco, but no United States marshal or other officials made a move. Henry George, then co-owner of the San Francisco *Daily Evening Post,* demanded prosecution, and he swore out a complaint in a federal court. The captain fled but was caught and brought to trial. The newspaper had offered a reward for his capture and it engaged a lawyer to fight the case. The captain was convicted, fined $5,000 and sentenced to prison for 14 months. George and the *Post* later took up other cases of maritime brutality and became known as champions of sailors' rights. George thundered against the force of law which kept the seamen bound according to their articles for long voyages. If all special statutes were to lapse, seamen would be "free to claim their wages and leave the ship whenever the anchor was down." This action would induce ship owners to provide decent food and conditions aboard ship, and it would give sailors equal footing with other workers in a free society to keep or change their jobs.

When Henry returned to Philadelphia he became a typesetter. At this time he encountered his first puzzling question in political economy.

An old printer had commented to him one day that wages are always low in old countries and high in new ones. The boy compared wages in the United States with those in Europe, and California's with those of the east coast. The old printer's words seemed true enough, but neither of them could explain why. The paradox stuck in Henry's mind and he continued to grope for an answer.

In the heated discussions of the slavery issue just prior to the Civil War, Henry took a strong anti-slavery stand. In this he opposed his parents, who supported peace, property rights and the Democratic Party.

The restless youth complained of low wages and intermittent employment in the printing trade. In 1857 he signed on as a seaman on a schooner carrying coal from Philadelphia to Boston. Times were even worse when he reached home again. He decided at age eighteen to leave for the west coast. The steamer *Schubrik* was heading for California as a light-house tender, and Henry signed on as a ship's steward, or storekeeper, at forty dollars a month. He started on the voyage on December 22, 1857, and he was not to return to his family in Philadelphia until eleven years later.

The chief incident of the voyage provided a bizarre tale written up by George and published in a Philadelphia weekly paper in 1866 and reprinted in a San Francisco journal. When the *Shubrick* left Rio de Janeiro, yellow fever broke out. All those who were stricken recovered except the second assistant engineer. As the young man knew he was dying, he pleaded to be buried ashore rather than at sea. The ship steamed up the La Plata River to Montevideo, and the captain asked permission to bury the corpse. Permission was denied, because quarantine regulations required that the ship go back some miles and commit the body to the sea.

The coffin, properly weighted, was slid overboard and it sank out of sight. As the *Shubrick* headed up the river again, the coffin rose to the surface. A boat was lowered, and some men tried to sink the box by fastening a small anchor and some heavy chain to it. The coffin seemed to elude their efforts in the fresh breeze and the choppy sea. After repeated efforts they succeeded in sinking the casket again. As George described the scene:

After waiting some time, to make sure that it could not float again, we started once more up the river, and this time awe was mingled with our grief. Most men who follow the sea have a touch of superstition. There is something in the vastness with which Nature presents herself upon the great waters which influences in this direction even minds otherwise sceptical. And as we steamed up the river, it was more than hinted among many of us that the strong desire of the dying man had something to do with the difficulty of sinking his body.[2]

The *Shubrick* again steamed up the La Plata past many naval and merchant vessels. The officer who boarded the ship directed that she go to the farther side of the harbor to lie in quarantine seven days before being allowed to take on coal. As the sun was sinking in the west, the startled crew saw an object floating in the distance and drifting toward them. It was the coffin they had sunk hours earlier. As if piloted by a live human being, the coffin turned and tacked past all the ships in the harbor, heading for the *Shubrick*. It touched the side of the vessel, halted a moment as if claiming recognition, and then slowly drifted past toward shore. The corpse was claiming burial on land! The crew buried their comrade on land, secretly, in the twilight; the dying wish was gratified.

The *Shubrick* reached San Francisco on May 27, 1858. Henry George, age nineteen, had arrived at his destination. Apparently then he jumped ship, losing his accumulated wages but buoyed with hope for the future.

The Young Man in California

Shortly thereafter Henry George worked his way as a seaman to British Columbia. The lure was the recent discovery of gold in the Frazer River region. He worked in a cousin's store in Victoria while waiting for the spring floods to subside. By the time he was able to go up river, discouraging reports about the prospects of finding gold sent him back to San Francisco "dead broke." He had an assortment of jobs as a typesetter, a weigher in a rice mill, a prospector for gold in California and a farm laborer. He looked forward eagerly to September 2, 1860, when he would be twenty-one years old and would qualify as a journeyman typesetter at full pay—if he could find a job.

---

2. *Ibid.*, p. 65.

As soon as he came of age, George joined the typographical union. He began to work irregularly as a substitute typesetter at a journeyman's wages. Then he joined the *California Home Journal* as foreman of the printshop. When the paper was sold, he was out of work again. He and five other printers bought the San Francisco *Daily Evening Journal.* The poverty of this enterprise was described later by George: "I worked until my clothes were in rags and the toes of my shoes were out. I slept in the office and did the best I could to economise, but finally I ran in debt thirty dollars for my board bill." The partnership was dissolved and George was again unemployed and penniless.

Shortly after his twenty-first birthday, George met Annie Fox at her seventeenth birthday celebration. She was an orphan, born in Australia but then living in California. Her uncle, Matthew McCloskey, was virtually her guardian after her grandmother died. As the young man courted the niece, her uncle wrote to Philadelphia to find out more about the George family; finding the lineage satisfactory, he permitted the courtship to continue. But Henry's loss of employment began to show in the growing shabbiness of his clothing. McCloskey finally told George that until he could show more evidence of prosperity, he should make his visits to Annie Fox less frequent. The young man replied with some anger, and the two hot-tempered men were about to come to blows when Annie rushed between them.

The next morning, when Henry came to see her, Annie announced that she would no longer live with her relatives in San Francisco; she would accept a teaching position in Los Angeles. Henry grieved at the thought of not seeing her again. He drew from his pocket a single coin and said, "Annie, that is all the money I have in the world. Will you marry me?" She answered, "If you are willing to undertake the responsibilities of marriage, I will marry you." They eloped that night, he in borrowed clothes that looked better than his own, and with borrowed money. She left home with one heavy package. It turned out to contain the *Household Book of Poetry* and all the other volumes that Henry had given her. He was twenty-two and Annie eighteen when they were married on December 3, 1861.

There was no wedding trip for them. The following morning Henry arose at five to go out and look for work. He was able to find a job as a substitute typesetter.

There followed years of precarious employment and poverty. On November 3, 1862 their first child, Henry George, Jr., was born; he was to be the first biographer of his father, and he was to serve as a representative in the United States Congress from New York. Their second child, Richard Fox George, was born on January 27, 1865; he was to become a noted sculptor, immortalizing his father in bronze. Between the births of their first two children, the Georges often were hungry. Henry would leave the house without breakfast, saying he would eat down town; but Annie knew he had no money. She would not complain, nor would she run up bills that she knew they could not pay. During her second pregnancy she parted with her little pieces of jewelry and trinkets until only her wedding ring (which had been her grandmother's) remained. Finally she told the milkman that she could no longer afford to take milk, but he offered to continue to supply it for printed cards, which she accepted. When Richard was born the doctor called out, "Don't stop to wash the child; he is starving. Feed him." Henry George, desperate for some money, described sixteen years later what happened that day:

I walked along the street and made up my mind to get money from the first man whose appearance might indicate that he had it to give. I stopped a man—a stranger—and told him I wanted $5. He asked what I wanted it for. I told him that my wife was confined and that I had nothing to give her to eat. He gave me the money. If he had not, I think I was desperate enough to have killed him.[3]

George later used this incident as proof that environment has more to do with human actions, and especially with so-called criminal actions, than we generally concede. Acute poverty, he said, may drive sound-minded moral men to commit evil deeds.

Things then began to improve somewhat. George found some work as a substitute typesetter, although it was scant and irregular. His wife paid part of the rent for their home by sewing for their landlady. The man of twenty-five was ready to begin his career as a writer.

George Becomes a Writer

Henry George began his career as a writer early in 1865, when he began practicing writing in order to improve his style. His first

3. *Ibid.,* p.149.

published piece was a long letter to the editor of a labor journal urging working men to think about political and social questions; they should discover if it is possible to "check the tendency of society to resolve itself into classes who have too much or too little."

His first published article was a fanciful sketch titled, "A Plea for the Supernatural," published in California and republished in Boston.

George was a substitute typesetter at the newspaper *Alta California* when the Civil War ended and Lincoln was assassinated. Anger ran high in San Francisco, and mobs destroyed several newspapers which had fostered secession. George, who had voted for Lincoln in 1860, led an assault against one of the "copperhead" newspapers, but when he got there others were already hurling type, furniture and machinery into the street, and little remained for him and his gang to do. The next day he wrote an impassioned eulogy of Lincoln called "Sic Semper Tyrannis!"; it was published by the newspaper he worked for. The beginning and ending paragraphs are worth quoting to show the passion and power of this fledgling writer:

A man rushed to the front of the President's box, waving a long dagger in his right hand, exclaiming, *"Sic semper tyrannis!"*

"Alta" despatches, April 15.

What a scene these few words bring—vivid as the lightning flash that bore them! The glitter and glare, curving circle and crowded pit, flash of jewels and glinting of silks—and the blanched sea of up-turned faces, the fixed and staring eyes, the awful hush—silence of death! . . .

Sic semper tyrannis! Blazoned on the shield of a noble State by the giants of the young republic, their degenerate sons shall learn its meaning! The murderer's shout as Lincoln fell, it will be taken up by a million voices. *Thus shall* perish all who wickedly raise their hands to shed the blood of the defenders of the oppressed, and who strive, by wickedness and cruelty, to preserve and perpetuate wrong. Their names shall become a hissing and a reproach among men as long as the past shall be remembered; and the great sin in whose support they spared no crime is numbered henceforth with the things that were. *Sic semper tyrannis!* Amen.[4]

A few days later the editor of the *Alta California* assigned George as

4. *Ibid.,* pp. 162-164.

a special reporter to describe the Lincoln mourning decorations throughout the city; this was the first writing for which he received payment. The printer had become a writer.

A little later George and his family moved to Sacramento, where he set type on a contract for official state government printing. After a year he returned to San Francisco, where a new daily paper, the *Times*, gave him a position in the composing room. Three of his editorial articles were accepted and published soon after the paper was founded on November 5, 1866. He became a reporter, an editorial writer, and by June, 1867 was managing editor. This was the year the Georges' third child, Jennie Teresa, was born; she lived until the year of her father's death, 1897, leaving a husband and a baby boy of seven months.

In August, 1868 George left the *Times* and became managing editor of the San Francisco *Chronicle*. In October he published his most important article up to that time: "What the Railroad Will Bring Us." It appeared in *The Overland Monthly,* a journal edited by Bret Harte, with Mark Twain among its .contributors. The first transcontinental railroad was nearing completion; in the face of widespread enthusiasm about this coming event, George raised doubts about the benefits it would bring. He had not yet hit upon the great theme he developed in *Progress and Poverty*. But in this article he did show his vast humanitarian concern about the poor, and he anticipated and deplored the widening gap between the rich and the poor that the railroad would bring.

The railroad will benefit only some people, said George. Those who have will become wealthier; those who have not will find it more difficult to make a living. Competition will reduce wages, and land prices will rise. The locomotive kills small towns and small businesses while it builds up great cities and great corporations.

Nor is it worth while to shut our eyes to the effects of this concentration of wealth. One millionaire involves the existence of just so many proletarians. It is the great tree and the saplings over again. We need not look far from the palace to find the hovel. When people can charter special steamboats to take them to watering places, pay four thousand dollars for the summer rental of a cottage, build marble stables for their horses, and give dinner parties which cost by the thousand dollars a head, we may know that there are poor girls on the streets pondering between starvation and dishonor. When liveries appear, look out for bare-footed children. A few liveries are now to be seen on our streets; we think their appearance coincides in date with the establishment of the almshouse. . . .

In the growth of large corporations and other special interests is an element of great danger. Of these great corporations and interests we shall have many. Look, for instance, at the Central Pacific Railroad Company, as it will be, with a line running to Salt Lake, controlling more capital and employing more men than any of the great eastern railroads who manage legislatures as they manage their workshops, and name governors, senators and judges almost as they name their own engineers and clerks![5]

During 1868-69 Henry George began his life-long personal struggle against the powerful and entrenched interests. The Associated Press and the Western Union Telegraph Company established a monopoly press service, excluding certain newspapers from access to their wire service. The San Francisco *Herald* engaged George to go to New York to try to get the paper admitted to the Associated Press; if that was refused, he was to establish his own news service for the paper. This assignment enabled George and his family to visit his Philadelphia relatives in 1868.

The Board of Directors of the Associated Press refused service to the *Herald.* George set up his own press bureau and telegraphed his dispatches through Western Union, which controlled the only route to San Francisco. George worked out a cooperative arrangement with the New York *Herald* news service, and the service he supplied his west coast paper was better than that of the Associated Press. Western Union then raised the San Francisco *Herald's* charges and lowered those of the Associated Press. This ended the rival news service and reestablished the monopoly, and it put the San Francisco *Herald* out of business.

While George was in the East, he wrote an article for Horace Greeley's *New York Tribune* opposing unrestricted Chinese immigration. This showed another side of George's character, racial intolerance, and it led to his exchange of letters with John Stuart Mill, the great English economist. George condemned the Chinese in the United States as "heathens, treacherous, sensual, cowardly and cruel. . . . Infanticide is common among them; so is abduction and assassination." West coast newspapers and unions hailed George's article and reprinted it with enthusiasm.

---

5. *The Overland Monthly,* Vol. 1, No. 4 (October, 1868), 303-304, 306.

George sent a copy of his *Tribune* article to Mill. The latter wrote a long letter in reply. He agreed with George that a large immigration must lower wage rates. But he wondered to what extent those who take possession of an area have the right to exclude the rest of mankind from moving in. Mill also thought that the character and habits of the Chinese in the United States could be improved. Aside from contract labor which he regarded as a form of slavery, Mill favored Chinese immigration.

George received much favorable publicity when he published Mill's letter in the Oakland *Daily Transcript,* of which he was then the editor.

While George was opposed to the most enlightened views of his time on the Chinese question, he was ahead of his time on women's rights. He published an editorial in 1872 saying that women have the capacity to fill the very highest positions in educational institutions, and they should get the same pay as men for performing the same duties equally well. He favored votes for women. His strong belief in feminism was indicated in behavior as well as in word. One day as he went home he saw his wife approaching from another direction. Catching sight of him she hurried up and explained, "I was delayed shopping. I'm sorry—I always like to be home waiting for you." "Annie," he responded almost severely, "don't you ever talk that way again. Just why must you get home at a certain time? I don't possess you! Never put me in the position, even in your thought, of being your master, to whom you need give an accounting of your actions! I'm free to come and go as I see fit—and so must you be!"[6]

Henry George, scholar, writer, social and political activist, and defender of the common man and woman, was now prepared to enter upon the greatest creative phase of his career. He began to develop the ideas that were to culminate in his masterpiece nine years later.

The Birth of Progress and Poverty

Henry George ascribed to a trifling incident the germination of his great idea. He was riding a horse in the open country in 1870, a few months after the completion of the transcontinental railroad.

---

6. Anna George de Mille, *Henry George, Citizen of the World* (Chapel Hill: The University of North Carolina Press, 1950), p. 69.

Absorbed in my own thoughts, I had driven the horse into the hills until he panted. Stopping for breath, I asked a passing teamster, for want of something better to say, what land was worth there. He pointed to some cows grazing off so far that they looked like mice and said: "I don't know exactly, but there is a man over there who will sell some land for a thousand dollars an acre." Like a flash it came upon me that there was the reason of advancing poverty with advancing wealth. With the growth of population, land grows in value, and the men who work it must pay more for the privilege. I turned back, amidst quiet thought, to the perception that then came to me and has been with me ever since.[7]

The following year George wrote his first analysis of the land question. His pamphlet, equivalent to about 150 ordinary book pages, he titled *Our Land and Land Policy, National and State.* This was to be expanded eight years later in his first and most famous book. As *Progress and Poverty* will be presented in the next two chapters, nothing more needs to be said at this point about his pamphlet, except that he had 1000 copies printed for $75; he sold 21 copies at 25 cents each, and the rest he gave away.

At the end of 1871, when Henry George was unemployed, he and two others became founding partners of the San Francisco *Daily Evening Post,* of which he was to become the editor. It was a crusading newspaper, supporting the taxation of land values to the exclusion of all other taxes. George was elected a delegate to the Democratic National Convention in 1872, and he and the paper supported Horace Greeley for president. Because George and his associates borrowed money to buy one of the best printing presses available, and could not meet the payments, the paper passed to other hands in 1875.

George had helped elect the Democratic governor of California. He asked that official "to give me a place where there was little to do and something to get, so that I might devote myself to some important writing." In January, 1876 he was given the office of State Inspector of Gas-Meters, which gave him the income and leisure to write his first and greatest book.

George was already well known on the west coast as an editor and a writer when he gave his first formal speech in 1876. It was in support of

---

7. Henry George, Jr., *The Life of Henry George,* p. 210.

Samuel J. Tilden, Democratic candidate for president, in opposition to Rutherford B. Hayes. He was asked to campaign throughout the state, and he became the leading Democratic orator in the presidential campaign. After the election George wrote to his mother: "I propose to read and study, to write some things which will extend my reputation and perhaps to deliver some lectures with the same view. And if I live I shall make myself known even in Philadelphia. I aim high."

On March 9, 1877 George gave, by invitation, a lecture to the students and faculty of the University of California at Berkeley; it was published in *The Popular Science Monthly* in March, 1880. There was talk of establishing a chair of political economy, and Henry George, this dropout from the first year of high school, was expected to fill it. His speech killed the chances of his appointment, for he was too honest and forthright to curb and bend his thoughts to the requirements of the job. Here are some of his thoughts that were well received by the students but disliked by the authorities of the University:

It seems to me that the reasons why political economy is so little regarded are referable partly to the nature of the science itself and partly to the manner in which it has been cultivated.

In the first place, the very importance of the subjects with which political economy deals raises obstacles in its way. The discoveries of other sciences may challenge pernicious ideas, but the conclusions of political economy involve pecuniary interests and thus thrill directly the sensitive pocket-nerve. . . .

And springing, as it seems to me, from the same fundamental cause, there has arisen an idea of political economy which has arrayed against it the feelings and prejudices of those who have most to gain by its cultivation. The name of political economy has been constantly invoked against every effort of the working classes to increase their wages or decrease their hours of labor. The impious doctrine always preached by oppressors to oppressed—the blasphemous dogma that the Creator has condemned one portion of his creatures to lives of toil and want, while he has intended another portion to enjoy "all the fruits of the earth and the fullness thereof"—has been preached to the working classes in the name of political economy, just as the "cursed-be-Ham" clergymen used to preach the divine sanction of slavery in the name of Christianity. In so far as the real turning [*burning?*] questions of the day are concerned, political economy seems to be considered by most of its professors as a scientific justification of all that is, and by the convenient formula of supply and demand they seem to mean some method which Providence has of fixing the rate of wages so that it can never by any action of the employed be increased. Nor is it merely ignorant pretenders who thus degrade the name and terms of political economy. This character has been so firmly stamped upon the science itself as currently held and taught that not even men like John Stuart Mill have been able to emancipate themselves. Even the intellectually courageous have shrunk from laying stress upon principles which might threaten great vested interests; while others, less scrupulous, have exercised their ingenuity in eliminating from the science everything which could offend those interests. Take the best and most extensively circulated text-books. While they insist upon freedom for capital, while they justify on the ground of utility the selfish greed that seeks to pile fortune on fortune, and the niggard spirit that steels the heart to the wail of distress, what sign of substantial promise do they hold out to the working man save that he should refrain from rearing children?. . .

For the study of political economy you need no special knowledge, no extensive library, no costly laboratory. You do not even need text-books nor teachers, if you will but think for yourselves. . . . Education is not the learning of facts; it is the development and training of mental powers. All this array of professors, all this paraphernalia of learning, cannot educate a man. They can but help him to educate himself. Here you may obtain the tools; but they will be useful only to him who can use them. A monkey with a microscope, a mule packing a library, are fit emblems of the men—and, unfortunately, they are plenty—who pass through the whole educational machinery, and come out but learned fools, crammed with knowledge which they cannot use—all the more pitiable, all the more contemptible, all the more in the way of real progress, because they pass, with themselves and others, as educated men. . . .

You are of the favored few, for the fact that you are here, students in a university of this character, bespeaks for you the happy accidents that fall only to the lot of the few, and you cannot yet realize, as you may by-and-by realize, how the hard struggle which is the lot of so many may cramp and bind and distort—how it may dull the noblest faculties and chill the warmest impulses, and grind out of men the joy and poetry of life; how it may turn into the lepers of society those who should be its adornment, and transmute into vermin to prey upon it and into wild beasts to fly at its throat, the brain and muscle that should go to its enrichment! These things may never yet have forced themselves on your attention; but still, if you will think of it, you cannot fail to see enough want and wretchedness, even in our own country today, to move you to sadness and pity, to nerve you to high resolve; to arouse in you the sympathy that dares, and the indignation that burns to overthrow a wrong.

And seeing these things, would you fain do something to relieve distress, to eradicate ignorance, to extirpate vice? You must turn to political economy to know their causes, that you may lay the axe to the root of the evil tree. Else all your efforts will be in vain. Philanthropy, unguided by an intelligent apprehension of causes, may palliate or it may intensify, but it cannot cure. If charity could eradicate want, if preaching could make men moral, if printing books and building schools could destroy ignorance, none of these things would be known today.[8]

George noted in his diary that on September 18, 1877 he began to write *Progress and Poverty.* The whole country was suffering an industrial depression at the time. Great railroad strikes were widespread, and troops and police were called out to run the trains. There were rioting, shooting, killing and the destroying of property in the great industrial conflicts that erupted. The unrest spread to California, and Henry George wrote with passion and outrage against poverty, hunger and the maldistribution of wealth and income in a country as rich as the United States.

On October 2, 1877 the Georges' fourth and last child was born. She was Anna Angela, the second child to write the father's biography. Her daughter, Agnes de Mille, became the famous dancer and choreographer.

By the end of 1877 hard times again appeared for the George family. Income had shrunk to almost nothing, because there were few uninspected gas meters left, and payment was on a piece-rate basis. George's debts amounted to $450, and he was able to eke out a living by delivering lectures.

In mid-March of 1879 Henry George completed *Progress and Poverty.* He was thirty-nine years old, and he had spent a year and a half writing his treatise. When he finished the last page late at night, he went down on his knees and wept with relief.

---

8. Henry George, *The Study of Political Economy* (New York: The Robert Schalkenbach Foundation, no date), pp. 4-7, 13-15.

CHAPTER 2

A Guide to Progress and Poverty

Henry George sent the manuscript of *Progress and Poverty* to D. Appleton and Company, Publishers, in New York City. They rejected it because they thought that sales of the book would not justify its publication. Other publishers in England and the United States also turned it down, including Harper and Scribner's.

George had the plates for the book made by a former partner who owned a printing shop. With this major expense covered by others, D. Appleton offered to publish the book. They thought so little of its financial prospects that they omitted applying for foreign copyrights. The book sold over two million copies in the United States, and it was translated and published in thirteen foreign languages.

The subtitle of *Progess and Poverty* shows the main direction of George's thoughts. It is "An inquiry into the cause of industrial depressions and of increase of want with increase of wealth. . . The remedy."

In the introductory chapter George pointed to the prodigious increase in man's wealth-producing capacity. Steam and electricity, improved processes and laborsaving machinery, the division of labor and large-scale production, the development of trade—all tremendously increased the productivity of labor. This increase aroused hopes for the elimination of poverty. But disappointment followed disappointment, the burden of toil was not reduced for those who most need it, and the poor remained poor. Society continued to be afflicted with depressions, unemployment, idle capital, financial difficulties among businessmen, and hard times for the workers. There is distress where large standing armies are maintained, and distress where they are not; distress where protective tariffs stupidly and wastefully hamper trade, and distress where trade is nearly free; there is distress under both autocratic and democratic governments; there is distress in countries with paper money and also in countries where gold and silver are the basis of the currency.

Seeking the common cause underlying all these problems under the most diverse conditions, George realized that the enormous increase of productive power does not overcome poverty or lighten the burdens of those compelled to toil. It simply widens the gulf between the rich and the poor. Material progress actually produces poverty. Squalor and misery, and the vices and crimes that spring from them, everywhere increase as the village grows into the city. It is in the older and richer sections of the United States that pauperism and distress among the working classes are becoming most painfully apparent. "This associ-ation of poverty with progress is the great enigma of our times." This was the paradox that George proposed to solve.

Book I.   *Wages and Capital*

"Why," asked George, "in spite of increase in productive power, do wages tend to a minimum which will give but a bare living?" He attacked the answer that political economists from Adam Smith to John Stuart Mill gave: the wages-fund theory. This doctrine held that wages are determined by the supply of and demand for labor. The supply depends on the number of people seeking work. The demand for labor depends on that part of the capital set aside for the payment of wages. No matter what the wage rate according to this theory, the same sum is expended for labor.

George denied the validity of this theory. He did not believe that wages depend upon the ratio between the amount of labor seeking work and the amount of capital devoted to its employment. If that were true, the relative abundance of labor would mean a relative scarcity of capital, and low wages would be associated with high interest rates. Conversely, the relative scarcity of labor and abundance of capital would result in high wages and low interest rates. Yet we find that high wages and interest go together, and so do low wages and interest. "Both wages and interest have been higher in the United States than in England, in the Pacific than in the Atlantic States," George declared.

The principle that George proclaimed was this: "That wages, instead of being drawn from capital, are in reality drawn from the product of the labor for which they are paid."

Land, labor and capital, said George, are the three factors of production. Land includes not merely the surface of the earth, but the whole material universe outside man himself. It includes ore in the ground, a waterfall that supplies power, and so on.

Labor means all human exertion, including the knowledge, skill and industry that people acquire.

Capital includes those things that are not either land or labor, but it results from the union of these two original factors of production. Capital covers such things as buildings, cattle, tools, machinery— man-made goods used for further production.

George's conclusion was that wages are not drawn from capital, but are produced by the workers. This is most obvious when the worker is self-employed. If one gathers birds' eggs or picks wild berries, the eggs or berries are the wages. If a worker makes shoes out of leather, the shoes are the wages, and they are not derived from capital. Even if a laborer works for an employer, "Production is always the mother of wages. . . . It is from the produce of labor, not from the advances of capital that wages come." Labor always precedes wages, for wages are paid only after the performance of work. The erroneous idea is that labor cannot exert its productive power unless supplied by capital with maintenance.

Bring the question to the test of facts. Take, for instance, an employing manufacturer who is engaged in turning raw material into finished products—cotton into cloth, iron into hardware, leather into boots, or so on, as may be, and who pays his hands, as is generally the case, once a week. Make an exact inventory of his capital on Monday morning before the beginning of work, and it will consist of his buildings, machinery, raw materials, money on hand, and finished products in stock. Suppose, for the sake of simplicity, that he neither buys nor sells during the week, and after work has stopped and he has paid his hands on Saturday night, take a new inventory of his capital. The item of money will be less, for it has been paid out in wages; there will be less raw material, less coal, etc., and a proper deduction must be made from the value of the buildings and machinery for the week's wear and tear. But if he is doing a remunerative business, which must on the average be the case, the item of finished products will be so much greater as to compensate for all these deficiencies and show in the summing up an increase of capital. Manifestly, then, the value he paid his hands in wages was not drawn from his capital, or from anyone else's capital. It came, not from capital, but from the value created by the labor itself. There was no more advance of capital than if he had hired his hands to dig clams, and paid them with a part of the clams they dug. Their wages were as truly the produce of their labor as were the wages of the primitive man, when, long "before the appropriation of land and the accumulation of stock," he obtained an oyster by knocking it with a stone from the rocks.[1]

What conclusion did George draw from this analysis? If wages are drawn, not from capital but from the produce of labor, we cannot alleviate poverty by increasing capital or restricting the number of laborers.

The question to be considered in Book II is: "Do the productive powers of nature tend to diminish with the increasing drafts made upon them by increasing population?" Having attacked the wages-fund theory that wages are determined by the ratio of capital to laborers, George now sought to demolish the theories of Thomas Robert Malthus.

Book II.   *Population and Subsistence*

Malthus believed that population tended to increase in a geometric ratio, doubling every twenty-five years. Subsistence that can be obtained from the land increases in an arithmetic ratio, increasing by a quantity equal to what it produced at the time Malthus was writing. Thus every twenty-five years population tends to increase as 1, 2, 4, 8, 16, 32, while food tends to increase at most as 1, 2, 3, 4, 5, 6. If these ratios are correct, people are bound to starve unless birth rates are lowered or death rates are raised. Falling birth rates can result, said Malthus, from abstinence from sexual intercourse or from vice; the latter included both prostitution and birth control. The death rates

1. Henry George, *Progress and Poverty* (New York: Robert Schalkenbach Foundation, 1971), pp. 60-61. [Originally published in 1879.]

could be raised by war, famine, misery and disease, which are nature's remedies for overpopulation.

The population theory of Malthus was based on the law of diminishing returns and was tied closely to the law of rent, which was of major concern to George. In this context the law of diminishing returns may be stated as follows: As more and more workers cultivate a given area of land, total output will increase, but the average output per worker will fall. The growth of both population and the labor force therefore reduces the subsistence available per person. The rising demand for farm products raises their prices, and these justify hiring the extra workers. As the last or marginal worker hired must cover his wages and other costs of production, the extra productivity of the other workers goes to the landowner in the form of rent. This illustrates rent arising at the intensive margin of cultivation.

The same thing happens at the extensive margin of cultivation. As population grows and the demand for farm products rises, prices rise. It then pays to work poorer and poorer land. At the margin of cultivation where the poorest land is worked, the return must cover labor and other costs of production. The extra productivity of the better land goes to the owner in the form of rent. Therefore as population grows, rents rise and wages remain at the minimum of subsistence or even below that.

George denied that there is a tendency for population to increase faster than subsistence. Population, he said, does not double every 25 years, and overpopulation is not a cause of poverty and hunger:

The Malthusian doctrine does not deny that an advance in the productive arts would permit a greater population to find subsistence. But the Malthusian theory affirms—and this is its essence—that, whatever be the capacity for production, the natural tendency of population is to come up with it, and, in the endeavor to press beyond it, to produce, to use the phrase of Malthus, that degree of vice and misery which is necessary to prevent further increase; so that as productive power is increased, population will correspondingly increase, and in a little time produce the same results as before. What I say is this: that nowhere is there any instance which will support this theory; that nowhere can want be properly attributed to the pressure of population against the power to procure subsistence in the then existing degree of human knowledge; that everywhere the vice and misery attributed to overpopulation can be traced to the warfare, tyranny, and oppression which prevent knowledge from being utilized and deny the security essential to production.[2]

Pauperism and starvation, said George, are caused by landlords who charge exorbitant rents. Tenant farmers have no incentive to improve the soil or increase their capital because the landlords will raise their rents. The producers of wealth work under conditions which deprive them of hope, of self respect, of energy and thrift. It is the injustice of society, not the stinginess of nature, that causes want and misery.

George denied the validity of the law of diminishing returns. Plants and animals multiply much more rapidly than human beings do; therefore there should be no shortage of food. Both the jayhawk and the man eat chickens, but the more jayhawks the fewer chickens, while the more people the more chickens there will be. People control and increase their own food supply. Since matter cannot be created or destroyed, life does not use up the forces that maintain life. "[T]he earth could maintain a thousand billions of people as easily as a thousand millions." With every increase in population, the new mouths to feed come with hands to work, and the efficiency of production grows, George declared:

I assert that, other things being equal, the greater the population, the greater the comfort which an equitable distribution of wealth would give to each individual. I assert that in a state of equality the natural increase of population would constantly tend to make every individual richer instead of poorer.[3]

It is obvious that wealth grows with population, not merely in the aggregate, but also on a per capita basis. Even if growing numbers of people require that poorer soil be worked, that is more than overcome by the growing efficiency of large numbers. Twenty men working together will, where nature is stingy, produce more than twenty times the wealth that one person can produce where nature is bountiful.

---

2. *Ibid.,* p. 123.
3. *Ibid.,* pp. 141-142.

George further declared:

The denser the population the more minute becomes the subdivision of
labor, the greater the economies of production and distribution, and,
hence, the very reverse of the Malthusian doctrine is true; and, within
the limits in which we have reason to suppose increase would still go
on, in any given state of civilization a greater number of people can
produce a larger proportionate amount of wealth, and more fully
supply their wants, than can a smaller number.

Look simply at the facts. Can anything be clearer than that the cause
of poverty which festers in the centers of civilization is not in the
weakness of the productive forces? In countries where poverty is
deepest, the forces of production are evidently strong enough, if fully
employed, to provide for the lowest not merely comfort but luxury.
The industrial paralysis, the commercial depression which curses the
civilized world today, evidently springs from no lack of productive
power. Whatever be the trouble, it is clearly not in the want of ability
to produce wealth.

It is this very fact—that want appears where productive power is
greatest and the production of wealth is largest—that constitutes the
enigma which perplexes the civilized world, and which we are trying to
unravel. Evidently the Malthusian theory, which attributes want to the
decrease of productive power, will not explain it. That theory is utterly
inconsistent with all the facts. It is really a gratuitous attribution to the
laws of God of results which, even from this examination, we may infer
really spring from the maladjustments of men—an inference which, as
we proceed, will become a demonstration. For we have yet to find what
does produce poverty amid advancing wealth.[4]

If overpopulation is not a cause of poverty and hunger, what is? This
is the crucial question that Book III sought to answer.

Book III. *The Laws of Distribution*

With material progress, wages fail to increase, and in fact tend to
decrease. Why? Each productive laborer produces his own wages instead
of drawing his wages from capital. As the number of laborers grows, the
efficiency of production increases and wages should rise. Low wages do
not come from the limited amount of capital or from the limited power
of nature. The cause of low wages is not to be found in the laws which

---

4. *Ibid.*, p. 150.

govern the production of wealth, but rather in the laws which govern distribution.

To find the law of wages, we must determine the laws which fix the share that goes as interest to the owners of capital, and the share that goes as rent to the owners of land. If the two shares are determined, the third share is the remainder of output or income that goes as wages to labor. Profits can be excluded, said George, because part of the profit is really wages—the wages of superintendence; part is interest on capital; and part is compensation for risk, and risks are eliminated when all the transactions of a community are taken together.

Rent, said George, is the price of monopoly; it arises from private ownership of a free gift of nature which human exertion can neither produce nor increase. He accepted David Ricardo's definition: the rent of land is determined by the excess of its produce over that which the same effort can produce from the least productive land in use. This law also applies to land used for other purposes than agriculture, and for other natural resources. Labor and capital get what they could have produced on the marginal, no-rent land. The extra productivity on the better land is taken by the landlord. In algebraic form:

$$\text{Produce} = \text{Rent} + \text{Wages} + \text{Interest}$$

$$\text{Therefore Produce} - \text{Rent} = \text{Wages} + \text{Interest}$$

Thus, said George, wages and interest do not depend on the output of labor and capital, but rather on what is left after rent is taken out. No matter how much productivity increases, declares George, if rent increases proportionally, neither wages nor interest can increase:

The increase of rent which goes on in progressive countries is at once seen to be the key which explains why wages and interest fail to increase with increase of productive power. For the wealth produced in every community is divided into two parts by what may be called the rent line, which is fixed by the margin of cultivation, or the return which labor and capital could obtain from such natural opportunities as are free to them without the payment of rent. From the part of the produce below this line wages and interest must be paid. All that is above goes to the owners of land. Thus, where the value of land is low, there may be small production of wealth, and yet a high rate of wages and interest, as we see in new countries. And, where the value of land is high, there may be a very large production of wealth, and yet a low rate of wages and interest, as we see in old countries.[5]

Wages depend on what labor could get on marginal land where no rent is paid. Where land is free and labor is unassisted by capital, the whole product goes to labor as wages. Where land is free and labor is assisted by capital, wages consist of the whole product less the necessary payment of interest to induce the saving that results in the accumulation of capital. Where land is owned privately and rent arises, wages are fixed by what workers can earn on marginal land that pays no rent. Finally, where land is all monopolized, competition among workers forces wages down to the minimum of subsistence. Wages may not fall in absolute levels, but they fall as a percentage of total output. The landlords get a rising share of the total output. The evidence is seen in rising land values as society progresses. "Rent swallows up the whole gain and pauperism accompanies progress," states George.

George then took a closer look at the distribution of wealth as society develops its productive power.

Book IV.   *Effect of Material Progress Upon the Distribution of Wealth*

George opened this book with two apt quotations from writers who were very much concerned with poverty, John Stuart Mill and Elizabeth Barrett Browning:

Hitherto, it is questionable if all the mechanical inventions yet made have lightened the day's toil of any human being.

—John Stuart Mill

Do ye hear the children weeping, O my brothers,
    Ere the sorrow comes with years?
They are leaning their young heads against their mothers,
    And that cannot stop their tears.
The young lambs are bleating in the meadows;
    The young birds are chirping in the nest;
The young fawns are playing with the shadows;
    The young flowers are blowing toward the west—

5. *Ibid.*, p. 172.

But the young, young children, O, my brothers,
    They are weeping bitterly!
They are weeping in the playtime of the others,
    In the country of the free.

—Mrs. Browning[6]

The conflict of interests is not, said George, between labor and capital; instead, it is between labor and capital on one side and landownership on the other. He agreed that the increasing pressure of population which compels the cultivation of inferior land does raise rents. But there are also other causes that raise rents. Any progress which increases production will redistribute wealth in favor of the landowners. The two trends that contribute to material progress are increases in population and improvements in the efficiency of production.

Increased population, even without any advance in technology, increases the productive power of labor. A thousand men will produce much more than ten times as much as a hundred men can. Even if poorer soil is worked as population rises, average output per person will not fall. Wage rates may rise, but the percentage of income that goes to labor will fall because landowners get a rising share.

According to George, rents rise with growing population even with no improvements in efficiency. Similarly, rents rise if efficiency improves even with no increase of population. With inventions and improvements, less labor and capital will be required to produce any given amount of output. As unemployment develops, wages and interest fall to some minimum level, and the share that goes to rent rises, declares George:

[A]s we can assign no limits to the progress of invention, neither can we assign any limits to the increase of rent, short of the whole produce. For, if laborsaving inventions went on until perfection was attained, and the necessity of labor in the production of wealth was entirely done away with, then everything that the earth could yield could be obtained without labor, and the margin of cultivation would be extended to zero. Wages would be nothing, and interest would be nothing, while rent would take everything. For the owners of the land,

---

6. *Ibid.*, p. 226.

being enabled without labor to obtain all the wealth that could be procured from nature, there would be no use for either labor or capital, and no possible way in which either could compel any share of the wealth produced. And no matter how small population might be, if anybody but the landowners continued to exist, it would be at the whim or by the mercy of the landowners—they would be maintained either for the amusement of the landowners, or, as paupers, by their bounty.

This point, of the absolute perfection of laborsaving inventions, may seem very remote, if not impossible of attainment; but it is a point toward which the march of invention is every day more strongly tending. And in the thinning out of population in the agricultural districts of Great Britain, where small farms are being converted into larger ones, and in the great machine-worked wheat fields of California and Dakota, where one may ride for miles and miles through waving grain without seeing a human habitation, there are already suggestions of the final goal toward which the whole civilized world is hastening. The steam plow and the reaping machine are creating in the modern world latifundia of the same kind that the influx of slaves from foreign wars created in ancient Italy. And to many a poor fellow as he is shoved out of his accustomed place and forced to move on—as the Roman farmers were forced to join the proletariat of the great city, or sell their blood for bread in the ranks of the legions—it seems as though these laborsaving inventions were in themselves a curse.[7]

Another evil of private landownership is the expectation of continually rising land values because of continually rising rents. This leads to speculation in land, withholding it from use or renting it for more money than is actually justified at the time. Many unused lots in cities are being withheld by their owners in anticipation of rising land prices. This works in a cumulative process, for withholding land raises its price, and rising prices create expectations of further increases. Rising rents are limited only by the minimum of subsistence that workers have to get in order to work and reproduce.

In the next book George was concerned with rents rising to the point where production is curtailed; this situation can be seen when depressions develop.

---

7. *Ibid.*, pp. 252-253.

Book V.   *The Problem Solved*

The main cause of periodic depressions, said George, is rising land values which cut down the earnings of labor and capital. But workers would not suffer unemployment and deprivation if they had access to the land. What prevents labor from employing itself on the land? Simply, that land has been monopolized and is held at speculative prices, based not on present value but on expected future value that will grow with growing population.

This explains why poverty and wealth exist together; why low wages go with high productivity; why interest and wages are higher in new than in older communities though both average and aggregate production is less. Improvements increase the productive power of labor and capital without increasing their rewards. There is no conflict of interest between labor and capital, but there is between them and the landowners, George writes:

Take . . . some hardheaded business man, who has no theories, but knows how to make money. Say to him: "Here is a little village; in ten years it will be a great city—in ten years the railroad will have taken the place of the stage coach, the electric light of the candle; it will abound with all the machinery and improvements that so enormously multiply the effective power of labor. Will, in ten years, interest be any higher?"

He will tell you, "No!"

"Will the wages of common labor be any higher; will it be easier for a man who has nothing but his labor to make an independent living?"

He will tell you, "No; the wages of common labor will not be any higher; on the contrary, all the chances are that they will be lower; it will not be easier for the mere laborer to make an independent living; the chances are that it will be harder."

"What, then, will be higher?"

"Rent; the value of land. Go, get yourself a piece of ground, and hold possession."

And if, under such circumstances, you take his advice, you need do nothing more. You may sit down and smoke your pipe; you may lie around like the lazzaroni of Naples or the leperos of Mexico; you may go up in a balloon, or down a hole in the ground; and without doing one stroke of work, without adding one iota to the wealth of the community, in ten years you will be rich! In the new city you may have a luxurious mansion; but among its public buildings will be an almshouse.[8]

Having laid the groundwork by explaining why poverty coexisted with progress, George was prepared to offer a remedy for the problem.

Book VI.   *The Remedy*

George said that there are six tendencies and policies which are believed to be reliable means to relieve poverty and distress. He saw little merit in them; he preferred his own "radical and simple" proposal. "Let us now consider what may be hoped for," he declared:

> I. From greater economy in government.
> II. From the better education of the working classes and improved habits of industry and thrift.
> III. From combinations of workmen for the advance of wages.
> IV. From the co-operation of labor and capital.
> V. From governmental direction and interference.
> VI. From a more general distribution of land.
> Under these six heads I think we may in essential form review all hopes and propositions for the relief of social distress short of the simple but far-reaching measure which I shall propose.[9]

First, what could be expected from greater economy in government? There might be some temporary benefit to the poorest people, but the saving would ultimately be swallowed up by the landowners. Government economy is desirable, but it can have no direct effect on overcoming poverty and increasing wages so long as land is monopolized.

Second, what will happen when there is a diffusion of education and improved habits of industry and thrift? Labor will not benefit. When land is all monopolized, rent must drive wages down to the minimum of subsistence. This being the case, industriousness, skill, frugality and intelligence can help some workers in competing with others; but as the average of all these virtues rises, average wages will not rise. If one

---

8. *Ibid.,* pp. 293-294.
9. *Ibid.,* p. 300.

individual works more hours than the average, he will increase his wages; but the wages of all cannot be increased in this way.

Third, what can unions do for workers? They can raise wages. This is not at the expense of other workers; nor is it at the expense of capital, for wages do not come from capital, but rather from current production of the workers. Higher wages come out of rent. The problem is that unions have only limited powers to raise wages. The more they succeed, the greater the pressures arise that bring wages back to the average level. If the printers' union raises wages ten percent, both the demand for and the supply of labor are affected. There will be less printing to do at the higher wage, and more workers will compete for the shrinking volume of work. If the wage increase is higher than ten percent, these tendencies to pull wages down are even stronger. Besides, the real antagonists are not labor and capital, but both on one side against landowners on the other. The final objection George had to unions was that they were necessarily tyrannical and strikes are destructive.

Fourth, can cooperatives remedy the grievances of the working classes? Since these grievances do not arise from any conflict between labor and capital, cooperatives cannot raise wages or relieve poverty. They can reduce the costs of doing business, as laborsaving machinery does, but both simply raise rent. If cooperatives were completely successful, they would eliminate the employing capitalists and greatly increase the efficiency of labor. The same amount of wealth would then be produced with less labor, and the owners of land could command a greater amount of wealth for the use of their land.

Fifth, what may be hoped for from more government regulation? "[W]hatever savors of regulation and restriction is in itself bad, and should not be resorted to if any other mode of accomplishing the same end presents itself," George declared. He even condemned the graduated income tax because it required the employment of many people who were given too much power. The income tax produces bribery, perjury and evasion, he said. It also weakens the incentive to accumulate wealth, which is one of the strong forces for industrial progress.

Sixth, would a more general distribution of land be helpful? Farms are growing larger, for machinery and large-scale production are superseding small-scale production. Therefore any measures which permit or facilitate the greater subdivision of land would be ineffective. In addition, to compel subdivision would mean to check production. If large farms are more efficient than small ones, they should be permitted to operate.

The real solution to poverty, said George, is to make land common property. The unequal ownership of land inevitably results in the unequal distribution of wealth. In the next book he developed and defended his basic solution.

Book VII. *Justice of the Remedy*

Land, said George, is a free gift of nature. The equal right of all men to the use of land is as clear as their equal right to breathe the air. Poverty, vice and misery are not due to overpopulation as Malthus said; they are due to private ownership of land. Labor needs land, and to deny labor's equal right to the use of land is to deny the right of labor to its own product. Landowners are unjustly enriched while everybody else is robbed.

Security of tenure is necessary to use the land, to improve it, to erect buildings, railroads and other structures on it, to dig out the minerals, and so on. If society were to confiscate rent for the benefit of the whole community, people could be allowed to keep the land they have.

If land were made common property, or if the rent of land were confiscated for the benefit of the whole community, should the present landowners be compensated for their losses? If the original appropriators of the land now lost their claim to the surpluses produced by society, that could be regarded as simple justice. But suppose someone bought land recently with money earned legitimately? He was paying for the right to receive annual rents. Should he be deprived of that income without compensation? Yes, said George. If the interests of the landholders are to be safeguarded, the general interests and general rights will be sacrificed. Because people were robbed in the past, should they suffer robbery in the future? The innocent purchaser of a wrongful title gets no claim or compensation for his mistake. Nobody should be compensated for the loss of annual income from the ownership of land.

How would George's proposal work if it were adopted? He analyzed this question in the next book.

Book VIII.   *Application of the Remedy*

What is required for the improvement of land is not absolute ownership of the land, but security for the improvements. Land is frequently improved by tenants, even in the construction of buildings on rented land. Payment of annual rent would be made to the government, not to individual owners, declared George:

> The complete recognition of common rights to land need in no way interfere with the complete recognition of individual right to improvements or produce. Two men may own a ship without sawing her in half. The ownership of a railway may be divided into a hundred thousand shares, and yet trains be run with as much system and precision as if there were but a single owner. . . .
>
> We should satisfy the law of justice, we should meet all economic requirements, by at one stroke abolishing all private titles, declaring all land public property, and letting it out to the highest bidders in lots to suit, under such conditions as would sacredly guard the private right to improvements.[10]

But it is not really necessary to confiscate land. All who now hold land would be permitted to retain the title to it. Let them continue to call it *their* land. It is only necessary to confiscate rent. Landowners may keep the shell of the nut if society takes the kernel. Some rent is already taken in taxation. All we need do is take all the rent and abolish all other taxes. Such a simple reform would raise wages, increase the earnings of capital, wipe out poverty, produce full employment, lessen crime, elevate morals and purify government, stated George:

> Tax manufactures, and the effect is to check manufacturing; tax improvements, and the effect is to lessen improvement; tax commerce, and the effect is to prevent exchange; tax capital, and the effect is to drive it away. But the whole value of land may be taken in taxation, and the only effect will be to stimulate industry, to open new opportunities to capital, and to increase the production of wealth.[11]

---

10. *Ibid.,* pp. 399, 403.
11. *Ibid.,* p. 414.

In the next book George examined the long-run effect of the single
tax on the rent of land.

Book IX.   *Effects of the Remedy*

George opened this book with a quotation from the Old Testament
vision of a better social order:

Instead of the thorn shall come up the fir tree, and instead of the
brier shall come up the myrtle tree.

And they shall build houses and inhabit them; and they shall plant
vineyards and eat the fruit of them. They shall not build and another
inhabit; they shall not plant and another eat.

—Isaiah

The present method of taxation inhibits energy, industry, skill, thrift
and world trade, George asserted:

If I have worked harder and built myself a good house while you have
been contented to live in a hovel, the taxgatherer now comes annually
to make me pay a penalty for my energy and industry, by taxing me
more than you. If I have saved while you wasted, I am mulct, while you
are exempt. If a man builds a ship we make him pay for his temerity, as
though he had done an injury to the state; if a railroad be opened,
down comes the tax collector upon it, as though it were a public
nuisance; if a manufactory be erected we levy upon it an annual sum
which would go far toward making a handsome profit. We say we want
capital, but if anyone accumulate it, or bring it among us, we charge
him for it as though we were giving him a privilege. We punish with a
tax the man who covers barren fields with ripening grain, we fine him
who puts up machinery, and him who drains a swamp. How heavily
these taxes burden production only those realize who have attempted
to follow our system of taxation through its ramifications, for, as I have
before said, the heaviest part of taxation is that which falls in increased
prices. But manifestly these taxes are in their nature akin to the
Egyptian Pasha's tax upon date trees. If they do not cause the trees to
be cut down, they at least discourage the planting.

To abolish these taxes would be to lift the whole enormous weight
of taxation from productive industry. The needle of the seamstress and
the great manufactory; the cart horse and the locomotive; the fishing
boat and the steamship; the farmer's plow and the merchant's stock,
would be alike untaxed. All would be free to make or to save, to buy or

to sell, unfined by taxes, unannoyed by the taxgatherer. Instead of saying to the producer, as it does now. "The more you add to the general wealth the more shall you be taxed!" the state would say to the producer, "Be as industrious, as thrifty, as enterprising as you choose, you shall have your full reward! You shall not be fined for making two blades of grass grow where one grew before; you shall not be taxed for adding to the aggregate wealth."[12]

Under this system of taxation wages would rise to the fair earnings of labor. Competition would no longer be one-sided as under the old system. Workers would no longer compete with each other for jobs and thereby cut wages down to the point of bare subsistence. The employers would not only compete among themselves for workers, but workers could become self-employed because land would no longer be monopolized. Labor and capital between them would receive the total output minus that part taken by the state. Even the tax on land values would be used for public purposes. Every increase in the efficiency of production would increase rent taken by the government. This would benefit every member of the community.

How will landowners fare, George asked, under the single tax? They are likely to be alarmed at the prospect, and they will play on the fears of owners of small farms and homesteads. But landowners will obviously benefit under this scheme if their interests as laborers or capitalists exceed their interests as landowners. They will have to pay more land taxes, but all other taxes will be terminated. Trade will improve, we will have full employment, and wages and interest will rise. Small farmers would gain enormously because the single tax would bear most heavily, not on farm land, but on urban land.

Even the large landowners would gain from the growing prosperity and improved social conditions brought about by the single tax, says George:

Thus to put all taxes on the value of land, while it would be largely to reduce all great fortunes, would in no case leave the rich man penniless. The Duke of Westminster, who owns a considerable part of the site of London, is probably the richest landowner in the world. To take all his ground rents by taxation would largely reduce his enormous income, but would still leave him his buildings and all the income from them,

12. *Ibid.,* pp. 434-435.

and doubtless much personal property in various other shapes. He would still have all he could by any possibility enjoy, and a much better state of society in which to enjoy it.[13]

What would the government do with the large and growing revenues from a 100 percent tax on rent? It could operate those enterprises that are run more efficiently as monoplies than as competitive enterprises, such as telegraphs, mail delivery, railroads and highways. The government could serve the public by providing public baths, museums, libraries, gardens, lecture halls, music and dancing halls, theaters, schools, shooting galleries, playgrounds, gymnasiums, and so on. Roads could be lined with fruit trees, and heat, light and water could be delivered free along the streets. Discoverers and inventors could be rewarded, and scientific research supported.

The last book of *Progress and Poverty* is called *The Law of Human Progress.* It is a philosophical, sociological and religious treatise which can be foregone in this summary of George's great work.

---

13. *Ibid.,* p. 452.

CHAPTER 3

Evaluation of
Progress and Poverty

In the previous chapter we summarized *Progress and Poverty* in the spirit of Henry George, without evaluating his arguments. In this chapter the author presents his judgments on the validity of George's analysis. In the next chapter we shall look at the public's reception of *Progress and Poverty* and George's views in general.

The Validity of Progress and Poverty

George was perceptive in denying the wages-fund theory. John Stuart Mill had already repudiated that doctrine in a British journal a few years earlier, but George undoubtedly was unaware of Mill's change of mind. It is not true that wages must make up a fixed and rigid part of the total capital available for investment. The theory was used as an anti-union argument. If the total sum available for wages is fixed, if some workers can win an increase of pay, less money will be available for other workers; therefore wage increases are gained, not at the expense of capitalists or landlords, but at the expense of other workers. But if the dividing line between wages and other incomes is changeable within certain limits, then workers as a whole can get a larger or smaller share of the national income, depending on their organized strength and bargaining position. George's attack on the wages-fund theory helped discredit a doctrine that was scientifically untenable and biased in favor of the class interests of employers.

George was correct in accepting and building upon the law of rent as developed by David Ricardo in 1815. He understood that rent arises from the extra productivity of the better soil compared with the marginal land, which pays no rent. The landowner is in a position to benefit from the surplus return of the more productive land. It is not

51

high rents that produce high prices of goods, but high prices of goods that result in high rents. High rents in turn result in high prices of land.

George also appreciated, more than Ricardo did, that significant increases in land prices and rents in urban areas overshadow by far agricultural rents. A store on the outskirts of a city might yield its owner a modest return. If it were located in the center of the city, suppose it would yield an extra $16,000 per year because of the larger concentration of shoppers. If eight percent were considered a reasonable return on such an investment in land, the land on which the store is built would be worth $200,000. Society will have created this value without any effort or wisdom exhibited by the owner of the land. The store owner renting this land would receive only the average rate of return, with the extra productivity of the land due to its location going to the owner. If the store owner also owned the land, his income would be partly rent, partly interest on his capital, partly wages for his labor, and partly profit.

As land is a free gift of nature to society, the landowner as landowner does nothing to earn his income. If he develops his own land, then he is entitled to the earnings of his labor and capital. But in his role as landowner he contributes nothing.

George was correct in showing that a one hundred percent tax on economic rent need not interfere with production at all. In fact, land resources would be used more fully and sooner under his scheme. Suppose a person owns a mansion on an acre of land in the center of a city, and he refuses to let anyone else use it. It could be determined by competitive bidding or by comparing this land with adjacent land in use that someone would give $100,000 a year to use this acre for business purposes. The landowner would have to pay a tax of $100,000 *per annum.* He would be free to continue to use that acre for his own exclusive pleasure, but he would have to pay its full rental value to the government. This would combine the maximum of individual freedom with the concept of justice and equity. In addition, few individuals would refuse to allow their land to be used because they did not like the new rules of Henry George's game. Their annual tax would be levied, not according to the economic rent actually produced by the land, but according to the economic rent it would generate if it were put to the highest use. Withholding land from use would be an expensive protest on the part of landowners.

This withholding urban land from use is more widespread than most people realize. The speculators hope to see large increases in land prices by leaving their land idle. Thus in the crowded city of San Francisco 23 percent of the usable land was undeveloped in 1955. In Los Angeles 65 percent of the suitable land was undeveloped for urban use in the same year. In Brooklyn the figure was 44 percent.[1]

George was right in saying that taxing away all economic rent need not interfere with production. Since land and other natural resources are a free gift of nature, and as their supply cannot be augmented or reduced (except through depletion or erosion), the same amount will be available for society's use whether it is taxed or not. George pointed out that large investments are made on rented land. This practice has reached the point where some large buildings are erected on rented land on 99-year leases. Who will own such a building when the lease on the land expires? The landowner, of course. Why is the tenant willing to accept such a situation and build on someone else's land? For two reasons. First, the building he puts up may be worthless after 99 years. Second, even if it is valuable, the power of compound interest, or the power of discounting future values to the present, is such that the present value of a payment due in 99 years is negligible.

To illustrate this idea, suppose a tenant is about to rent a piece of land for 99 years. He plans to put up an office building for twenty million dollars, and he guesses that at the end of the lease it will still be worth a million. He is about to sign the lease when the shadow of a doubt crosses his mind, and he says to the landowner: "Why should my descendants give your descendants a million-dollar property 99 years from now? I demand compensation for the building that I will put up and the owner of the land will then get for nothing."

The landowner may well reply: "I agree that your building will be worth a million dollars in 99 years. But the present value of this future sum, discounted at a reasonable six percent, is only $3,124. I'll give you that sum now. If you put it away at six percent compounded annually, it will be worth a million dollars in 99 years."

This is the situation that makes feasible the large investments that are being made on rented land. The ownership of land is not a prerequisite to its development.

The validity of George's view can be seen in the fact that the land under Number One Wall Street in New York City has sold for $700 a

---

1. U. S. Department of Agriculture, *Land. The Yearbook of Agriculture, 1958* (Washington, D. C.: Government Printing Office, 1958), p. 515.

square foot or 30.5 million dollars an acre. Land in downtown Tokyo was worth $200 a square foot in 1971. The Disney interests secretly acquired 27,500 acres in Florida for their Disney World and related enterprises for an average of $185 an acre. Since then commercial interests have paid up to $300,000 an acre for the best locations close to the Disney gates. Even the air can be sold; an option on air over the Pennsylvania Railroad tracks in New York City was worth more than three million dollars an acre in 1955. A Times Square billboard brings in 15 thousand dollars a year. These examples illustrate society's tribute to the landowners who do nothing as landowners to satisfy the needs of society; they extract tribute under the protection of the law.

An average acre of cultivated farmland was worth $11 in 1850, $20 in 1900, $65 in 1950, and $195 in November 1970.[2]

Let us look at the total value of all the privately held land in the United States excluding Hawaii and Alaska. Unfortunately these figures are not available for the years before 1900, and they exclude the value of subsoil assets, which are considerable. We find that in 1900 the land was worth 27 billion dollars. By 1958 it was worth almost 11 times as much—290 billions. By 1968 privately held land almost doubled again in value, to 571 billion dollars.[3] This trend can be expected to continue.

No wonder Adam Smith in his *Wealth of Nations* (1776) said that landlords "love to reap where they never sowed."

Is the Landlords' Share Rising and Labor's Falling?

George was wrong in believing that wages probably would fall as society progresses, and the percentage of the nation's income that goes to labor certainly would fall; he was just as wrong in believing that the share going to landowners would increase.

As we noted above, in 1900 the value of the privately held land in the United States, excluding subsoil assets, was 27 billion dollars; the gross national product (GNP) was 17 billions. This means that the value of the land amounted to 159 percent of GNP. In 1958 the land was worth 290 billions and the GNP was 444 billions; the value of land

2. *Agricultural Situation,* Vol. 55, No. 4 (May 1971), 5.
3. U. S. Department of Commerce, *Historical Statistics of the United States, Colonial Times to 1957* (Washington, D. C.: Government Printing Office, 1960), p. 151; U. S. Department of Commerce, *Statistical Abstract of the United States, 1971* (Washington, D. C.: Government Printing Office, 1971), p. 328.

added up to 65 percent of GNP. In 1968 the land was worth 571 billion dollars, and the GNP was 865 billions; therefore the land was worth 66 percent of GNP. The value of land depends on the annual economic rent that it yields plus the speculative anticipation of future increases in rent; it is therefore safe to say that if the value of land as a percentage of the nation's income is not rising, the share of income going to landlords is not rising.

It has been observed that the share of the nation's income going to labor is quite stable from decade to decade. There can be no doubt that the absolute income of workers, measured by the purchasing power of their wages, is rising. In this it keeps pace with the growing efficiency of production. We can feel much dissatisfaction with the distribution of income, with the extremes of poverty and wealth, with how the national income is spent, with the disadvantages of a mindless concentration on growth, and so on. But George, like Marx before him, was wrong in believing that the absolute impoverishment of the workers was likely to occur, and that the relative impoverishment (compared to other groups) was inevitable.

How did George stumble into this erroneous analysis? It was easy: it stemmed from his mistaken notion that landowners are monopolists. If this were true, the landowner, with all the force of law and order imposed by the government, could say to the workers: "If you wish to use my land, I will allow you enough for you and your family to subsist. If you refuse my terms, you will starve to death. If your output increases, I will take the increase and leave you your minimal subsistence share."

But the landowners are not monopolists, even though they would like to be. There are literally millions of them in the United States and in other rich countries, and they are subject to competition among themselves as well as competing with buyers and renters of land. The next section will show how the landowners' share could fall with the growing efficiency of production.

Landowners, however, do act like monopolists in most countries in Asia, Africa and Latin America. They have a preponderance of economic and political power, and they use it to rackrent and exploit the peasantry. The majority of the people have few alternatives for earning a living, and they must work the land they do not own or they will starve. In addition to exorbitant rent, the ruling elite charge the peasants usurious interest rates on the credit they need. Prices for the goods that tenant farmers or sharecroppers buy and sell are manipulated to their disadvantage. In such countries Henry George's program would be like a breath of fresh air in an oppressive and stifling atmosphere. (But it will take more than persuasion and a majority of the ballots to break the power of the dominant oligarchy.)

George's Confusion of the Law of Diminishing Returns, Increasing Returns to Scale, and Growing Efficiency

It is understandable that George, writing almost a hundred years ago, confused these concepts which then were not very well understood.

It simply is not true, as George claimed, that the earth could support a thousand billion people as easily as one billion. He was confusing increasing returns to scale and growing efficiency with the law of diminishing returns. These three principles are valid, and the first two offset the third to a considerable extent. We shall treat them separately in order to analyze how they work.

We shall first look at the law of diminishing returns. Assume a fixed quantity of land and a state of technology that does not change. Suppose the labor of one worker and $100 of capital are applied to grow 10 acres of wheat. The yield is, say, 100 bushels. If there were no law of diminishing returns, two workers and $200 of capital could produce 200 bushels on the same 10 acres. A thousand workers and $100,000 of capital could produce 100,000 bushels. A million workers and $100 million of capital could produce 100 million bushels of wheat. If there were no law of diminishing returns, all the wheat for the whole world could be grown on the 10 acres of land. This, of course, is preposterous. As labor and capital are added to a fixed quantity of land, the total output will increase, but the average output per unit of labor and of capital will fall.

The law of diminishing returns is offset but not refuted by improvements in technology and growing efficiency. Suppose in the above example this year one worker and $100 of capital produce 100 bushels of wheat on 10 acres. Next year a new and better variety of wheat is planted, and two workers and $200 of capital produce 300 bushels. In the third year a new method of fertilization is developed, and three workers and $300 of capital produce 500 bushels. With each improvement the average output per worker and per $100 of capital rises. This is the trend that refuted the Malthusian pessimism about overpopulation.

But does improving technology invalidate the law of diminishing returns? It does not. Within the framework of any technology, the law of diminishing returns operates. In the above example, suppose we take the third year, when three workers and $300 of capital produced 500 bushels of wheat. To keep technology constant, let us consider different alternatives during that third year. Perhaps one worker and $100 of capital could produce 250 bushels; two workers and $200 of capital could produce 400 bushels; three workers and $300 of capital could produce 500 bushels; four workers and $400 of capital could produce 550 bushels. This illustrates increasing total output and falling average output as labor and capital are increased on a fixed quantity of land.

Which of these opposing tendencies will predominate? Either, depending on the circumstances. If population is growing very rapidly and if technology is improving slowly, the law of diminishing returns will predominate; food prices will rise, rents will rise, and wages will be at the minimum of subsistence or below. If, however, population increases slowly and technological advances are rapid, food prices and rents will not rise much. This is what has happened in agriculture in the United States. It helps explain why we spent 27.9 percent of our disposable personal income on food in 1909, 23.5 percent in 1929, 24.8 percent in 1957, and 15.9 percent in March 1972.[4]

Of course we would expect people to spend a smaller share of their incomes on food as their incomes rise. In addition, farmers produce nonfood commodities as well. Let us compare the change in prices of all the goods and services farmers buy and the change in prices of all the things they sell. We find that taking 1910-14 as 100, the farmers were paying an average of 415 for the things they bought in November 1971; they were receiving 290 for the things they sold. That is, the cost of their purchases rose 315 percent, while the price of their farm products rose 190 percent. This means that in November, 1971, a typical basket of farm products could buy 70 percent of what it would have bought in 1910-14. This tells us that farm products are relatively cheaper than they used to be and that rents are not absorbing the economic surplus as George thought they would.

The following tables will explain further the law of diminishing returns, the effects of improved technology, and how rent arises.

Assume that we have a small isolated community that has 100 acres

---

4. Computed from *Historical Statistics of the United States, Colonial Times to 1957,* pp. 139, 178, 179; *Agricultural Situation,* Vol. 56, No. 5 (June 1972), 14.

of each grade of land A through D, as shown in Table 1 below. If we
were to treat all the land in the same way, we would get 20 bushels per
acre of grade A land, 15 bushels on grade B, and so on.

We define the $10 input for each acre as that return which will give
the tenant farmer an average rate of return that is adequate enough to
keep him in farming. Ten dollars will cover the cost of his seed,
fertilizer, wear and tear on his machinery, and so on; the sum will also
compensate him for his labor, interest on his invested capital, and profit
for being a risk-taker in his farm enterprise.

As long as the population and the demand for wheat are small, only
the best land will be used, the price of wheat will be 50¢ per bushel,
and there will be no rent, as shown in line 1 of the table. With the
growth of population, 2,000 bushels are produced on the 100 acres of
grade A land, and this becomes inadequate to meet the demand. The
price therefore rises to 66 2/3¢ as seen in line 2 of Table 1, and now it
pays to work grade B land, which yields 15 bushels per acre. This land
produces no rent because it is marginal land that just barely

TABLE 1

**Rent Measured from the Extensive Margin of
Cultivation**

Price of Wheat per Bushel	Rent per Acre Derived from Each Grade of Land			
	A	B	C	D
	Input $10 Yield 20 bu./acre	Input $10 Yield 15 bu./acre	Input $10 Yield 10 bu./acre	Input $10 Yield 5 bu./acre
$ .50	0			
$ .66 2/3	$3.33	0		
$1.00	10.00	$5.00	0	
$2.00	30.00	20.00	$10.00	0

compensates the tenant farmer for his efforts and investment. But grade
A land now produces a surplus, yielding $13.33 per acre. Tenants will
be eager to rent grade A land for the extra return it will produce.
Competition among them will lead to a rental payment to the
landowner of $3.33.

We now have 2,000 bushels being produced on the 100 acres of grade A land, and 1,500 bushels on grade B land when all of those 100 acres are used. As population grows, they require more wheat, and the price rises to $1 per bushel. Now grade C land can be worked as the marginal no-rent land, as is apparent in line 3 of Table 1. Grade B land produces a surplus of $5 per acre which goes to the landowner as rent, leaving the tenant farmer with the average rate of return. The wheat from grade A land also sells for a dollar a bushel, and the rent is $10 per acre.

When the 100 acres of grade C land is all farmed, it produces 1,000 bushels. When the total demand for wheat at $1 per bushel exceeds 4,500 bushels, the price of wheat in this example rises to $2, making it just barely profitable to work grade D land. The rent rises, as shown in the bottom line of Table 1, to $30 per acre on grade A land, $20 on grade B, and $10 on grade C. Thus do landowners grow rich.

Let us assume now that through improved technology we can produce twice as much wheat as before with the same expenditure of labor and capital. This is illustrated in Table 2. We can now produce 4,000 bushels on the 100 acres of grade A land, 3,000 bushels on grade B land, and 2,000 bushels on grade C land, or 9,000 bushels in all, excluding grade D. In Table 1 we assumed a demand for up to 5,000 bushels at $2 per bushel, and all four grades of land will be worked. In Table 2 we see that with improved technology the price of wheat drops to 50¢. While more wheat will be wanted at the lower price, there is room for increased production from 5,000 bushels under the old conditions at $2 to 9,000 bushels under the new conditions at 50¢. The total rent in line 4 of Table 1 is $3,000 for 100 acres of grade A land, $2,000 for 100 acres of grade B land, and $1,000 for 100 acres of grade C land, or $6,000 in all. Under the new conditions assumed in Table 2, total rent has fallen to $1,000 on grade A land and $500 on grade B, or a total of $1,500. This illustrates what had prevented landowners from getting an ever-increasing share of the nation's income as predicted erroneously by Henry George. Since there are no known limits to the improvement of efficiency, this can be expected to continue in the future. His analysis was based on the assumption that the landowners act as a monopoly. If we abandon this assumption, his analysis becomes fallacious. Rents tend to rise with the growing demand for farm products, and they tend to fall with the growing efficiency of production.

TABLE 2
Rent Measured from the Extensive Margin of Cultivation
with Improved Technology

Price of Wheat per Bushel	Rent per Acre Derived from Each Grade of Land		
	A	B	C
	Input $10 Yield 40 bu./acre	Input $10 Yield 30 bu./acre	Input $10 Yield 20 bu./acre
$0.50	$10	$5	0

We can combine Tables 1 and 2 in hypothetical Table 3, which illustrates both the Malthusian pessimism based on the law of diminishing returns and George's optimism based on improved technology. Here we are looking only at grade A land, which is subject to diminishing returns as the land is worked more intensively by investing more labor and capital per acre.

TABLE 3

Diminishing Returns and Improved Technology

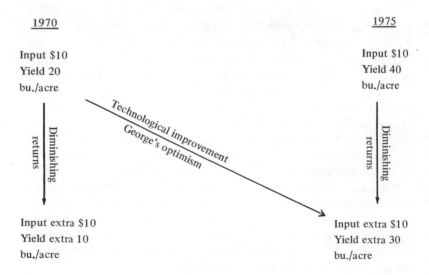

<u>1970</u>   <u>1975</u>

Input $10   Input $10
Yield 20   Yield 40
bu./acre   bu./acre

Input extra $10   Input extra $10
Yield extra 10   Yield extra 30
bu./acre   bu./acre

In any one year, keeping technology constant, the more labor and capital we invest per acre, the larger the total output but the smaller the average output per unit of labor and capital invested. But with technological improvement over a period of time, the average output per unit of labor and capital tends to increase. That is how we can feed a growing population better than in the past. George was perceptive in predicting this trend, but he was wrong in thinking it would necessarily tend to increase rents.

There remains one further point to discuss in this section. That is George's view that

increased population, of itself, and without any advance in the arts, implies an increase in the productive power of labor. The labor of 100 men, other things being equal, will produce much more than one hundred times as much as the labor of one man, and the labor of 1,000 men much more than ten times as much as the labor of 100 men; and, so, with every additional pair of hands which increasing population brings, there is a more than proportionate addition to the productive power of labor.[5]

This idea, which has been developed more fully since George's day, has come to be called "increasing returns to scale." It tells us that if all factors of production are increased together, the efficiency of production increases. It is very obvious in certain types of economic activity. A large circulation of newspapers and books, for example, lowers the cost per copy. A large radio and television audience is cheaper to serve per 1,000 listeners or viewers than is a small audience. The growth of population increases the efficiency of a railroad up to a certain point. It is also true of manufacturing. Large factories are more efficient than small ones. Suppose you have a factory with 100 workers and a million dollars of capital. If you increase labor and capital by 10, you will increase output by more than 10. But this process cannot go on indefinitely. If we had a factory as large as a county, it would be terribly inefficient.

There probably are increasing returns to scale in agriculture up to a certain point, for large farms are more efficient than small farms. But a farm the size of a whole state would be very inefficient, for beyond a

---

5. *Progress and Poverty,* p. 232.

certain point there is nothing to be gained from increased size, and much to be lost. There is another difference between agriculture and industry that vitiates George's analysis. In industry one can increase all factors of production. In agriculture, once all the land is taken into use, labor and capital can be expanded but not land. That is where the law of diminishing returns becomes significant. If one factor—land—is kept constant, and the other factors have increased, the *average* output per unit of increasing factor must eventually decrease. Had George understood this, he would not have made the preposterous statement that the earth could support a thousand billion people as easily as one billion. Only phenomenal, and as yet unseen, improvements in technology could make this possible.

We shall now look at whether or not the single tax would be adequate for all government expenditures.

The Inadequacy of the "Single Tax"

Henry George contended that if a 100 percent tax on economic rent were enacted, no other taxes would be necessary; the government would have ample funds to meet its expenses and to expand social services. This was certainly true in his day. But what has happened since then?

As we saw above, in 1900 all the privately held land in the United States, excluding subsoil wealth, was worth 27 billion dollars. If we assume that land generated a six percent return on its value, the single tax would have produced 1.6 billion dollars of revenue each year. This is exactly what all levels of government—federal, state and local—were spending per year. The "single tax" would have worked even as late as 1900.

In 1968 the privately held land was worth 571 billion dollars. At six percent return, this means that all levels of government would have had 34 billion dollars to spend in 1968. The federal government actually spent 166 billion dollars that year, and state and local governments spent 116 billions, bringing the total to 282 billion dollars. Apparently the tax on economic rent would have generated only 12 percent of government requirements.

In fairness to George it must be granted that he would not admit this simple-minded comparison of single tax revenues and current expenditures as valid. He believed that his fundamental reform would unleash productivity and growth, thereby increasing government revenues and decreasing expenses. Production would increase, poverty would disappear, wages would rise, full employment would be attained, prices of goods would fall, and so on. With a world at peace, military spending could be eliminated and the federal government would have saved 81 billion dollars out of the 166 billions it spent in 1968. George hoped that his reform would enable us to eliminate welfare expenditures, police, prisons, customs houses, most tax collectors, and so on. Rising wealth and reduced poverty would generate increased government revenues from the tax on rent, and reduced expenditures.

It is very doubtful whether George's panacea would solve most of the problems of poverty and the maldistribution of income. The private ownership of capital is a more powerful cause than the private ownership of land in explaining the uneven distribution of income in industrial societies. In the next section we shall analyze his peculiar views of capitalism that led to his conclusion that his reform would turn laissez-faire capitalism into a utopia.

George's Misconceptions About the Nature of Capitalism

As shown early in Chapter 2 of this book, George argued that wages are drawn from the product of labor and not from capital. What are the implications and consequences of this view?

Writing *Progress and Poverty* during 1877-79, George developed his ideas at the very beginning of the epoch of big business in the United States. Instead of looking at the new situation that was arising around him, he looked backward at a society of craftsmen, small scale producers who were serving mainly local markets. A shoemaker draws his wages from the sale of his shoes in the village. A carpenter is paid by his neighbors for whom he works.

With the development of commercial and industrial capitalism, however, a greater length of time and greater distances are required between the production of raw materials and the sale of the finished products. The construction of a shoe factory or a steel mill does require a large outlay of capital to erect buildings, buy machinery, pay workers, stock inventory, and fill orders on perhaps 30 days' credit before any receipts are realized. We are all aware of the importance of accumulating capital in order to expand production.[6]

How could George overlook such an important principle? Aside from viewing producers as primarily small craftsmen using very little capital, he made another major error; this can be seen in the following quotation:

In short, as the payment of wages is always conditioned upon the rendering of labor, the payment of wages in production, no matter how long the process, never involves any advance of capital, or even temporarily lessens capital. It may take a year, or even years, to build a ship, but the creation of value of which the finished ship will be the sum goes on day by day, and hour by hour, from the time the keel is laid or even the ground is cleared. Nor by the payment of wages before the ship is completed, does the master builder lessen either his capital or the capital of the community, for the value of the partially completed ship stands in place of the value paid out in wages. There is no advance of capital in this payment of wages, for the labor of the workmen during the week or month creates and renders to the builder more capital than is paid back to them at the end of the week or month, as is shown by the fact that if the builder were at any stage of the construction asked to sell a partially completed ship he would expect a profit.[7]

George's error lay in his failure to distinguish between the *creation of value* by the worker and the *conversion of value into cash* by the capitalist through the sale of the product. Of course the worker has to produce, to increase value, before he is paid. But if years will elapse

---

6. In fairness to George, it should be pointed out that in a work published four years after *Progress and Poverty* he wrote that large farms are displacing small family farms, just as large businesses are displacing small craftsmen. See his *Social Problems,* Robert Schalkenbach Foundation, 1966, pp. 227-228. [Originally published in 1883.] He also referred to large-scale agriculture pushing people out of farming, as seen in Chapter 2 above in the quotation from pages 252-253 of *Progress and Poverty.* His ideal society seemed to be one in which a working man could establish himself on a small farm and make a living. In that sense he was looking backward at a Jeffersonian agrarian democracy and not ahead at the problems of industrial society.

7. *Progress and Poverty,* p. 67.

before the worker's product is sold for cash, then capital is required to finance the investment, including the means of subsistence for the worker and his family.

George held that Adam Smith misled political economy into the idea that capital employs labor and pays wages:

> But when we consider the origin and natural sequence of things, this order is reversed; and capital instead of first is last; instead of being the employer of labor, it is in reality employed by labor. There must be land before labor can be exerted, and labor must be exerted before capital can be produced. Capital is a result of labor, and is used by labor to assist it in further production. Labor is the active and initial force, and labor is therefore the employer of capital.[8]

Can we imagine a wage earner working for General Motors or Du Pont or International Business Machines telling the chairman of the board that he, the worker, is employing capital? That the role of capital is insignificant? That there is a harmony of interest between both sides? And that their mutual antagonist is the owner of the land on which the factory is built?

George's view that labor was independent of capital fitted well with his predilection in favor of solving all of labor's problems with the single tax. He believed that under his scheme every worker could, if he wanted to, establish himself on the land, which would no longer be monopolized. Employers would then have to offer high wages to attract workers. This optimism was negated by George's own view that farms were increasing in size because the larger farms were more efficient. George overlooked the fact that a certain amount of capital was necessary even to establish a small farm. After the Homestead Act was passed during the Civil War, settlers in the west could each get 160 acres free except for some filing fees. Few urban wage earners took advantage of this opportunity. It typically required $1,000 or more to acquire livestock and equipment and to feed a family for a year until the first crop came in; few workers could save that much out of the 10 or 15 dollars a week they earned. It is most unlikely that George's single tax would solve labor's problems so suddenly and completely. But if he

---

8. *Ibid.,* p. 163.

admitted that labor is ineffective without an accumulation of capital with which to work, his remedy would be weakened considerably.

As shown in Chapter 2 above, George manipulated his equation on the distribution of income to show a harmony of interest between labor and capital:

$$Produce - Rent = Wages + Interest$$

He could just as easily have shown the antagonism between labor on one side and landlords and capitalists on the other:

$$Produce - (Rent + Interest) = Wages$$

Had he chosen not to ignore profit, he might have written:

$$Produce - (Rent + Interest + Profit) = Wages$$

But this equation would not have suited his view of society. It implies the concepts of class struggle and anticapitalism, both of which George rejected.

George's naive optimism concerning the beneficence of his plan can be seen in his own words:

The monopoly of the land gone, there need be no fear of large fortunes. For then the riches of any individual must consist of wealth, properly so-called—of wealth, which is the product of labor, and which constantly tends to dissipation, for national debts, I imagine, would not long survive the abolition of the system from which they spring. All fear of great fortunes might be dismissed, for when every one gets what he fairly earns, no one can get more than he fairly earns. How many men are there who fairly earn a million dollars?[9]

Perhaps George is right: few men fairly earn a million dollars *(per annum?).* But wealth begets wealth through interest, profits and capital gains; the second million dollars are more easily acquired than the first. Without unions, which George did not believe to be very effective or desirable, and without government intervention in the economy, the

9. *Ibid.,* p. 453.

gap between rich and poor would grow wider. The ownership of capital gives far more wealth and power to a small group of people than the ownership of land. George was attacking one aspect of our great social problems while neglecting the others.

One of George's key theses was that high wages and high interest occur together, as do also low wages and low interest. This is a dubious generalization. One difficulty in testing this proposition is that the rate of interest should include only the reward for saving and not the payment to compensate for the riskiness of investment; this may be difficult to ascertain. Apparently in most of the poor counties wage rates are low and interest rates are high; this condition can be attributed to the abundance of labor, the scarcity of capital, and the fact that economic and political power is concentrated in the hands of the wealthy. The interest rates in Great Britain were higher and wage rates lower in the eighteenth century than in the twentieth century. The United States may have been unique in that wages and interest were both high early in our history because labor and capital were both scarce while natural resource supplies were abundant. In the depressed 1930's both wages and interest were low because both labor and capital were unemployed.

Voltaire's criticism of a single tax on rent is also appropriate to George's idea. The French physiocratic school advocated a one-third tax on rent because they believed only agriculture is productive enough to produce a surplus, an increase in value. Any other tax would be passed on to the landowner who would ultimately pay it. Voltaire, in his satire *The Man with Forty Crowns,* which was translated and published in English in 1768, pictured the wealthy merchant escaping all taxes; his poor nephew who owned his own land had to pay taxes on the 40 crowns ($25) annual income he had from the rent received from the land. Voltaire has the uncle saying to the nephew, "Pay then you, my friend, who enjoy quietly the net and clear revenue of forty crowns; serve your country well, and come now and then to dine with my servants."

CHAPTER 4

The Public's Reception of Henry George and Progress and Poverty

Progress and Poverty probably had the greatest circulation of any nonfiction book in the English language before 1900 except for the Bible. An official of the Robert Schalkenbach Foundation of New York City (which keeps George's books and pamphlets in print) reports that seven to eight thousand copies of *Progress and Poverty* are still sold each year.

People of the most disparate views can be found among the supporters of George, and the same is true of his opponents. His supporters include conservatives who welcome his laissez-faire views that government should play a minimal role in regulating or controlling business. Some conservatives also are enthusiastic about his demand that there should be no taxes except on land. His defense of businessmen's profits rings sweetly in their ears. Many liberals and radicals also support George's ideas. They are opposed to landowners receiving the "unearned increment" of land values produced by society and appropriated by the owners. Rising rents and land prices contribute to the inequality of income that they deplore.

Many conservatives oppose George's ideas because of his attack on landed property. He would in effect have the state confiscate land without any compensation at all. Perhaps the frightening thought occurs to them that if a government can expropriate the landowners, what is to prevent it from going further and seizing industrial and commercial property without payment? Most radicals, especially socialists and communists, oppose George because he didn't go far enough. He was clearly against seizing the wealth of capitalists and

68

landlords other than the land itself. He would not regulate or tax the rents paid for apartments or business properties. He would not try to use taxes to reduce the income gap between capitalists and workers. He was a staunch defender of a reformed capitalism.

George was a world-famous and controversial figure, and the literature about him is too vast to survey thoroughly.[1] All we shall do here is to sample some of the support and opposition that he found in the public arena.

Public Support for Henry George and Progress and Poverty

Millions of people throughout the world read and agreed with *Progress and Poverty.* Tens of thousands listened to his speeches and applauded enthusiastically his six lecture tours in the British Isles, and in Australia, Canada, and throughout the United States. Sixty-eight thousand men in New York City voted for him for mayor in 1886. A hundred thousand or more people passed his bier, or tried to, in a final tribute to the man they loved.

Many famous people were influenced by George and endorsed his views. The most notable in Asia was Sun Yat-sen, the father of the Chinese republic, who said, "I intend to devote my future to the promotion of the welfare of the Chinese people as a people. The teachings of Henry George will be the basis of our program of reform."

One of George's most distinguished European converts was Count Leo Tolstoy, who challenged private property in land. He came across George's book and was converted. He read *Progress and Poverty* to his peasants, and he wrote to some of the members of the Russian government and to the Czar himself advocating the abolition of landownership and the institution of the single tax in Russia.

John A. Hobson, English liberal reformer and anti-imperialist, said in 1897 that George exercised a more directly formative and educative influence over British radicalism since 1882 than any other man.

Professor John Dewey said in 1927:

It would require less than the fingers of the two hands to enumerate those who, from Plato down, rank with Henry George among the

1. One of the best Henry George collections is at the New York Public Library. It was given to the library by his daughter, Anna George de Mille, in 1925.

world's social philosophers. . . . No man, no graduate of a higher educational institution, has a right to regard himself as an educated man in social thought unless he has some first-hand acquaintance with the theoretical contribution of this great American thinker.[2]

Professor Eric F. Goldman had this to say about George's major work:

For some years prior to 1952, I was working on a history of American reform and over and over again my research ran into this fact. An enormous number of men and women, strikingly different people, men and women who were to lead twentieth century America in a dozen fields of humane activity, wrote or told someone that their whole thinking had been redirected by reading *Progress and Poverty* in their formative years. In this respect no other book came anywhere near comparable influence, and I would like to add this word of tribute to a volume which magically catalyzed the best yearnings of our grand-fathers and fathers.[3]

Tom L. Johnson, monopolist and social reformer, supported Henry George politically and financially with enthusiasm; he dedicated his autobiography, *My Story,* "To the Memory of Henry George." An inventor and entrepreneur, he acquired street railways in Cleveland, Indianapolis, Brooklyn, St. Louis, Detroit and other cities. In 1883 he came across *Social Problems* and *Progress and Poverty* and was immediately converted. Two years later he sought out George and told him he couldn't write or speak, but he could make money and devote it to publicize George's doctrines. Johnson bought several hundred copies of George's new book *Protection or Free Trade,* and sent one to every clergyman and lawyer in Cleveland.

George suggested that Johnson go into politics, which he did by winning a seat in the United States House of Representatives in 1890. During his two terms there he proclaimed that he was a monopolist and as long as he continued in business he would take advantage of all the class legislation enacted by Congress; but as a member of Congress he

---

2. Edward J. Rose, *Henry George* (New York: Twayne Publishers, Inc., 1968), p. 8.
3. Steven B. Cord, *Henry George: Dreamer or Realist?* (Philadelphia: University of Pennsylvania Press, 1965), p. 242.

would work, speak and vote against such class legislation. In opposing monoplies he was very much in the spirit of George.

Johnson together with five other congressmen had the entire 332 pages of George's *Protection or Free Trade* inserted in the *Congressional Record.* It was then reprinted for less than a cent a copy and mailed without a postage charge under the congressmen's franking privilege. A total of 1,200,000 copies were distributed in this way, and another 200,000 copies of a better, two-cent edition were also sent out; Johnson paid most of the printing costs. The total circulation of this book was almost two million copies in less than eight years.

During a tariff debate in Congress, George sat in the gallery of the House of Representatives and listened to his disciple Johnson—a steel rail manufacturer—make a fervent free trade speech and move to put steel rails on the free list. One protectionist Democratic representative called attention of the House to the master in the gallery and the pupil on the floor. Many of the free trade Democrats immediately streamed upstairs to shake hands with the man who held no political office but was an outstanding leader of the free trade forces.

Johnson was mayor of Cleveland from 1899 to 1909. He advocated votes for women and a more democratic system of government. He supported the legislative process known as the initiative, which permits the people to introduce or even enact laws. He favored the referendum, which means that measures passed by the legislative body must be submitted to the vote of the electorate for approval or rejection. The system of recall, which he advocated, means that a public official may be removed from office by a vote of the people. Johnson defended the municipal ownership of street railways. He supported George's tax policy by getting high assessments on land in Cleveland and low assessments on buildings. Antimonopoly laws, he said, were easy to evade; all legislation is futile if it doesn't strike privilege at its root which is the monopoly of land.

The Knights of Labor, a federation of unions organized in 1869, favored George's views. He had been a member of the Knights, and his ideas were included in their declaration of principles after 1884:

The land, including all the natural sources of wealth, is the heritage of all the people, and should not be subject to speculative traffic. Occupancy and use should be the only title to the possession of land.

Taxes should be levied upon its full value for use, exclusive of
improvements, and should be sufficient to take for the community all
unearned increment.[4]

Albert Jay Nock is an example of an extreme conservative who
endorsed George's views. He referred to "our enemy, the state," and his
attitude is similar to that of many right-wing supporters of George.
Nock wrote:

George the philosopher of freedom, George the exponent of individual-
ism as against Statism, George the very best friend the capitalist ever
had, George the architect of a society based on voluntary cooperation
rather than on enforced cooperation—this George, the truly great, the
incomparable George, sank out of sight, leaving only George the
economic innovator, the author of a new and untried method of laying
taxes.[5]

George's opposition to government had an altogether different
rationale from that of conservatives like Nock. His was rooted in a
radical critique of the role of the state. This is brought out forcefully in
a work published four years after *Progress and Poverty:*

It behooves us to look facts in the face. The experiment of popular
government in the United States is clearly a failure. Not that it is a
failure everywhere and in everything. An experiment of this kind does
not have to be fully worked out to be proved a failure. But speaking
generally of the whole country, from the Atlantic to the Pacific, and
from the Lakes to the Gulf, our government by the people has in large
degree become, is in larger degree becoming, government by the strong
and unscrupulous.
    The people, of course, continue to vote; but the people are losing
their power. Money and organization tell more and more in elections.
In some sections bribery has become chronic, and numbers of voters
expect regularly to sell their votes. In some sections large employers
regularly bulldoze their hands into voting as *they* wish. In municipal,
State and Federal politics the power of the "machine" is increasing. In
many places it has become so strong that the ordinary citizen has no
more influence in the government under which he lives than he would

4. Albert Jay Nock, *Henry George* (New York: William Morrow & Company,
1939), p. 183.
5. *Ibid.,* p. 215.

have in China. He is, in reality, not one of the governing classes, but one of the governed. He occasionally, in disgust, votes for "the other man," or "the other party;" but, generally, to find that he has effected only a change of masters, or secured the same masters under different names. And he is beginning to accept the situation, and to leave politics to politicians, as something with which an honest, self-respecting man cannot afford to meddle. . . .

In our National Senate, sovereign members of the Union are supposed to be represented; but what are more truly represented are railroad kings and great moneyed interests, though occasionally a mine jobber from Nevada or Colorado, not inimical to the ruling powers, is suffered to buy himself a seat for glory. And the Bench as well as the Senate is being filled with corporation henchmen. A railroad king makes his attorney a judge of last resort, as the great lord used to make his chaplain a bishop.[6]

George also differed from his conservative supporters by favoring government ownership and operation of monopolies such as railroads, telephone and telegraph systems, the supplying of gas, water, heat and electricity. Businesses that are in their nature monopolies, he said, are properly the functions of the state.

George's Conflict with Herbert Spencer

In *A Perplexed Philosopher* (his last book to be published during his lifetime) Henry George reviewed his conflict with Herbert Spencer, British philosopher and sociologist. In *Social Statics,* published in 1850 (29 years before *Progress and Poverty*), Spencer had condemned the private ownership of land. Existing titles to land are not legitimate, he declared, for they derive from violence, force, fraud and the claims of superior cunning. Sale or bequest do not generate a right to the present owners where it did not previously exist.

While Spencer did not take a clear stand on compensation for landowners, he firmly advocated the nationalization of the rental income from land:

"But to what does this doctrine, that men are equally entitled to the use of the earth, lead? Must we return to the times of uninclosed wilds,

6. Henry George, *Social Problems* (New York: Robert Schalkenbach Foundation, 1966), pp. 16-18. [Originally published in 1883.]

and subsist on roots, berries, and game? Or are we to be left to the management of Messrs. Fourier, Owen, Louis Blanc, and Co.?"

Neither. Such a doctrine is consistent with the highest state of civilization; may be carried out without involving a community of goods; and need cause no very serious revolution in existing arrangements. The change required would simply be a change of landlords. Separate ownerships would merge into the joint-stock ownership of the public. Instead of being in the possession of individuals, the country would be held by the great corporate body—Society. Instead of leasing his acres from an isolated proprietor, the farmer would lease them from the nation. Instead of paying his rent to the agent of Sir John or his Grace, he would pay it to an agent or deputy of the community. Stewards would be public officials instead of private ones; and tenancy the only land tenure.[7]

George alleged that between 1850 and 1882 nothing more was heard from Spencer on the land question. The first English edition of *Social Statics* was a small one, and it took ten years to sell all the books. The British landed interests could therefore overlook Spencer's attack, declared George:

But beyond the warnings that this was no way to success, which he doubtless received from friends, there is no reason to think that this revolutionary utterance of Mr. Spencer in "Social Statics" brought him the slightest unpleasant remonstrance at the time or for years after. If "Sir John and his Grace"—by which phrase Mr. Spencer had personified British landed interests—ever heard of the book, it was to snore, rather than to swear. So long as they feel secure, vested wrongs are tolerant of mere academic questioning; for those who profit by them, being the class of leisure and wealth, are also the class of liberal education and tastes, and often find a pleasing piquancy in radicalism that does not go beyond their own circles. A clever sophist might freely declaim in praise of liberty at the table of a Roman emperor. Voltaire, Rousseau and the encyclopedists were the fashionable fad in the drawing-rooms of the French aristocracy. And at the beginning of this century, and for years afterwards, a theoretical abolitionist, provided he did not talk in the hearing of the servants, might freely express his opinion of slavery among the cultured slaveholders of our Southern States. Thomas Jefferson declared his detestation of slavery, and, despite amendment, "writ large" his condemnation of it in the Declaration of Independence

---

7. Quoted in Henry George, *A Perplexed Philosopher* (New York: Robert Schalkenbach Foundation, 1965), pp. 8-9. [Originally published in 1892.]

itself. Yet that declaration was signed by slaveholders and read annually by slaveholders, and Jefferson himself never became unpopular with slaveholders. But when the "underground railway" got into operation; when Garrison and his colleagues came with their demand for immediate, unconditional emancipation, then the feeling changed, and the climate of the South began to grow hot for any one even suspected of doubting the justice of the "peculiar institution."

So it was with private property in land for over thirty years after "Social Statics" was written. One of the first to congratulate me on "Progress and Poverty," when only an author's edition of a few hundred copies had been printed, and it seemed unlikely to those who knew the small demand for works on economic questions that there would ever be any more, was a very large landowner. He told me that he had been able freely to enjoy what he was pleased to term the clear logic and graceful style of my book, because he knew that it would be read only by a few philosophers, and could never reach the masses or "do any harm."

For a long time this was the fate of Mr. Spencer's declaration against private property in land. It doubtless did good work, finding here and there a mind where it bore fruit. But the question had not passed beyond, and Mr. Spencer's book did not bring it beyond the point of extremely limited academic discussion.[8]

Social Statics was reprinted in the United States, where it sold well as Spencer's reputation grew. But in 1882 he prohibited the further import into Great Britain of his United States edition, even though he continued to receive royalties on his book's sales in the United States. He repudiated his earlier position on land in a letter to a newspaper, in magazine articles, and finally in a revised and abridged edition of *Social Statics,* published in England in 1892. George alleged that the new edition eliminated everything that might "offend vested interests."

The Opposition of Prominent Economists

In London Arnold Toynbee delivered two lectures criticizing Henry George in January, 1883; they were published later that year by Kegan Paul, Trench & Company.

Toynbee used radical arguments to promote his conservative viewpoint. Large farms, he said, hurt the farm laborers, and George

---

8. *Ibid.,* pp. 44-45.

would not touch the large-farm system. As Karl Marx and others pointed out, large businesses are stamping out small ones. Gradually capital is being accumulated in fewer and fewer hands, and some day we may have a handful of stupendous monopolists and a struggling mass of laborers at their feet. This, said Toynbee, is one great cause affecting the division of income; it is one great reason why wages have not risen in proportion to the increase in productive capacity.

What is the remedy? asked Toynbee. George offers none because he believes that once the state confiscates rent, individual interests will harmonize with the common interest; also competition, which we know is often baneful and destructive, will then become a beneficent force.

Toynbee argued that the age of government regulation has come. Factory acts do and should regulate the labor of men as well as women and children. The distribution of wealth can be improved by the state.

The confiscation of rent, said Toynbee, would produce a war between the classes and thereby divide the nation. Instead, we should support unions; cooperative production, especially in small scale trades; the right of farm laborers to buy houses, and to buy or rent a half acre of land; progressive taxation for both land and income. The British aristocracy is responsible and would respond to appeals to a sense of justice. There should be more social insurance through the "Friendly Societies" of the workers with a minimum of state aid. "The way we have got reforms carried in England is not by, as a rule, class war, but by class alliance."

Toynbee reported that he had two classes at his lectures, the poor and rich. Some workers, he said, interrupted him with revolutionary outcries.

Alfred Marshall, the world-famous marginalist or neoclassical economist, delivered three lectures on *Progress and Poverty* on February 19, 26, and March 5, 1883 in Bristol, England. These speeches were reported in the Bristol newspaper *Times and Mirror.*

Marshall criticized George for claiming that progress drives a wedge into the middle of society, raising those who are above it but lowering those who are below it. If the concept of a wedge is correct, most workers are above the wedge, for progress is pushing them upward, though unfortunately at a very slow rate. The lowest stratum, the pauper class, is being pushed downward, and this is a disgrace to the age. But *"pauperism is the product of freedom."* Slaves, like horses, are well fed, but free men may not be.

The division of income between capital and labor, said Marshall, depends on their relative scarcity. In new countries capital and labor are both scarce, and their earnings are high. As capital and labor grow more plentiful, their earnings fall. If population is plentiful and capital scarce, interest is high and wages low; the converse is also true.

People can go into business for themselves, and tens of thousands of working men had done so, many of them becoming employers. Large capitalists work for the smallest proportionate returns. They also have to get their best administrators from working men "because experience showed that business ability scarcely ever lasted three generations, and many fortunes were dissipated by the successors of those who made them."

If the original landholders had no good right to the land, Marshall argued, it would be wrong to punish the present owners, many of whom are descendants of workingmen who bought the land with the sweat of their brows. If rich men are prevented from investing in land, they will buy up railways and newspapers as they do in America; they would thereby "exercise a power which, if less conspicuous, might be far more injurious to the public interest than that of English landlords can possibly be."

Marshall was against the 100 percent tax on rent because it would ruin numberless poor widows and others who have invested their little all in land; society would be convulsed, with a danger of civil war; capital and business ability might be driven out of the country. If these things happened, the English working man, instead of being the best paid and the heartiest in Europe, might become almost the worst paid and the weakest.

How can the lowest classes be helped? asked Marshall, He had five proposals.

1. Workers should not marry so much earlier than the middle classes do, and they should save money before they marry. They should raise their children better. Emigration would help, and the State should educate the children.

2. Workers should put down the paupers who are lazy, vicious and deceptive. Public and private charity should be offered if necessary to upright, industrious and thrifty workers.

3. The government should increase the vigor of its factory and sanitary inspection. But hopefully before long the workers will be able to manage their own affairs with very little of such aid.

4. Workers should learn from the economists that it is selfish and wrong to curtail production in one trade, as through strikes, for it injures all other trades.

5. Workers should develop a higher sense of duty; this would save money and time spent in excessive drinking and crime.

Marshall's concern, as stated above, that George's proposal would ruin numberless poor widows, was also voiced by others. Exactly a year after the Marshall lectures, George spoke in Glasgow, on February 18, 1884. His speech, titled "Scotland and Scotsmen," was brilliant, and the audience received it with the greatest enthusiasm. During the question period, a man asked about the widows and orphans who receive interest on bonds secured by land. George's reply to that question may be considered a reply to Alfred Marshall:

Do not be deluded by this widow and orphan business. That is a matter that is always put to the front. When men talked about abolishing slavery in my country, the cry was raised about the widow and the orphan. It was said, "Here is a poor widow woman who has only two or three slaves to live upon; would you take them away?" It reminds me of the story of the little girl who was taken to see a picture of Daniel in the lions' den. She began to cry very bitterly, and her mother said, "Do not cry, do not cry; God will take care that no harm will befall him." To which she replied, "I ain't crying for him, but for the poor little lion in the back—he is so little I am afraid he won't get any." I propose to take care of the widows and the orphans. As I told those people in London whom I addressed recently, every widow, from the highest to the lowest, could be cared for. There need be no charity or degradation; every one of them could have an equal pension. It will only take twenty million pounds to give every widow in the three kingdoms a pension of £100. And in the state of society which would ensue from breaking up land monopoly, no one need fear that the helpless ones he left behind would come to want. This is not the case now.

Francis A. Walker was professor of political economy at Yale

University, later president of the Massachusetts Institute of Technology, and the first president of the American Economic Association. He wrote a popular textbook called *Political Economy* (3rd edition, 1888) in which he discussed George's theoretical views on rent. But of George's practical proposal to tax away all economic rent, Walker asserted: "I will not insult my readers by discussing a project so steeped in infamy."

A meeting to discuss the single tax was held at Saratoga, New York, on September 5, 1890. One of the addresses was by Professor Edwin R. A. Seligman of Columbia College, outstanding authority on taxation. He said that the desirability of the single tax should be tested against the three chief principles of good taxes: universality, equality and justice.

Many people, he said, would not be taxed in George's system, including the owners of corporate securities and business properties. It would therefore violate universality and equality. In addition, most landowners bought their land recently, and the whole preceding "unearned increment" has been capitalized into the swollen selling price of the land. Therefore existing owners should be compensated. "Any other plan would be sheer confiscation."

Justice, said Seligman, requires that ability to pay should be the basis of taxation. Land rent is no satisfactory index of this ability to pay.

Henry George attended this conference, and he made the following remarks:

Professor Seligman has said that the true principle is, not taxation according to benefits, but taxation according to ability,—meaning, I presume, ability to pay. To us it is as unjust and absurd to charge men with taxation in proportion to their ability to pay as it would be to charge them for postage-stamps in proportion to their ability to pay. If men get rich dishonestly, it is no remedy to tax them more. If they get rich honestly, it is a gross outrage. No one ought to be forced to pay more than another because he is more industrious or more talented, or has more foresight, or any other personal quality. All men ought to be put upon an equality of opportunity, letting whoso can work best and hardest take all the advantage that those qualities give. It is unjust to tax men according to their ability to pay. . . .

Professor Seligman said that the advocates of the single tax do not understand the science of finance. Well, if some of the reasoning we have heard here be the result of understanding the science of finance, we single tax men are glad that we don't understand it. He has also said that the professors of political economy as a class are against us. Unfortunately, that is true. But is it astonishing? Given a great social wrong that affects the distribution of wealth, and it is in the nature of things that professors of political economy should either belong to or consciously or unconsciously be influenced by the very class who profit by the wrong, and who oppose, therefore, all means for its remedy. . . .

Let me say a direct word to you professors of political economy, you men of light and leading, who are fighting the single tax with evasions and quibbles and hair-splitting. We single tax men propose something that we believe will make the life of the masses easier, that will end the strife between capital and labor, and solve the darkening social problems of our time. If our remedy will not do, what is your remedy? It will not do to propose little goody-goody palliatives, that hurt no one, help no one, and go nowhere. You must choose between the single tax, with its recognition of the rights of the individual, with its recognition of the province of government, with its recognition of the rights of property, on the one hand, and socialism on the other. . . .

Modern society cannot stand still. All over the civilized world social conditions are becoming intolerable. If you reject the single tax, look to it, from what you turn and toward what you are going. We propose to respect to the full the rights of property. We propose to assure to each man his own, be it much or little. We would remove all restraints on production, all penalties on honest acquisition. We care not how rich any man may become, so long as he does not appropriate what belongs to others. We ask no class legislation, no favors or doles for any set of men. We would do away with all special privileges, abolish all monopolies, and put all men on the same level with regard to natural opportunities and before the law. We would simplify government, do away with its interferences in private affairs, and strike at the root of political corruption.[9]

The Opposition of The New York Times

Many editorials in *The New York Times* denounced George and his ideas, but sometimes grudging credit was given for his courage,

---

9. F. B. Sanborn (ed.), *The Single Tax Discussion Held at Saratoga September 5, 1890,* reported for the American Social Science Association (Concord, Mass.: October 1890), pp. 82, 84-86.

integrity, honesty and sincerity. Three editorials appearing in almost a quarter of a century are representative.

It cannot be denied that Mr. Henry George has the courage of his convictions, such as they are. At a meeting of Churchmen—of all others—held in London yesterday, he is reported to have declared that as a matter of abstract justice no compensation should be awarded to the present landowners when their land shall have been "nationalized.". . . What he proposes is robbery out-and-out. . . . There is no right of property recognized in civilized communities which rests on a firmer foundation than that in land, and Mr. George must be a very dull observer if he does not see that there could be no form of robbery more gross and oppressive than that which would be perpetrated by the "Government" under pretense of serving "public purposes."[10]

The following editorial appeared six months after George's powerful campaign for mayor of New York City:

Ever since society has been organized on an industrial basis it has been fairly well understood that the conditions of prosperity in the world were industry and frugality. Those grew rich above their neighbors who worked harder and denied themselves more sternly than their neighbors. The average condition has been that of living from hand to mouth, as the saying is, simply because the average man has refused to do more work than would supply his immediate needs, and has been incapable of the self-denial required to make provision for the future. Those who have fallen below the average and have become burdens upon the workers of the community have done so because they have been incapable of even the average of industry and self-denial. Whether they are disabled in mind or body from doing their share of the world's work, or willfully shirk it, the result is the same.

Of course there are exceptions. As there are men who are poor by unmerited calamity, so there are men who grow rich by fraud. But the truth that prosperity comes from hard work and self-denial and that proverty is the result of laziness and self-indulgence is none the less patent to every man and woman in the United States. It is a lesson which experience teaches them daily, and it is a most wholesome and useful lesson. It is the real explanation and the only explanation of "Progress and Poverty," and it is recognized to be so by everybody who does not delude himself or is not deluded by others.

Nevertheless it is an explanation very distasteful to those who are

---

10. *The New York Times,* September 21, 1882, p. 4.

discontented with their lot and who find it bitter to admit that their fortunes correspond to their deserts. As these persons comprise almost all mankind, a man who offers another explanation by which prosperity is made irrelevant to merit, not as the exception, but as the rule, is sure of an eager hearing, even from those whose own experience emphatically contradicts his teachings. He appeals, in the first place, to that envy which is one of the meanest of human sentiments, and of which those who cherish it have generally the grace to feel ashamed. . . .

Upon educated persons who do not spend much of their time in envying those who are richer than themselves the panacea for poverty prescribed by Mr. Henry George has made no impression. They declare that his diagnosis of society is incorrect and his remedy preposterous; that the possession of even great riches by one man is neither on the face of it nor in fact an injury to another who does not possess them, and that inequality of fortune is not "wrong" in any sense in which inequality of intellect is not wrong, or a deluge or a drought or any other operation of nature.[11]

In 1905 followers of Henry George celebrated the twenty-fifth birthday of *Progress and Poverty* at a banquet at Hotel Astor in New York City. Among the two hundred and fifty present and paying homage to the memory of George were William Jennings Bryan, Edwin Markham, William Lloyd Garrison, Hamlin Garland, Louis F. Post, Ernest Thompson Seton, Lincoln Steffens, Ida M. Tarbell and Samuel R. Seabury. *The Times* reported the meeting and editorialized as follows:

It was necessary and natural that much high-sounding solemn nonsense should be talked at the Henry George-Bryan dinner. If that component had been omitted, the occasion would have been destitute of the characteristic single-tax flavor.[12]

Socialist Criticisms of George

While most conservatives accused George of going too far in his proposal to confiscate all ground-rent, the socialists accused him of not going far enough.

11. *Ibid.*, May 5, 1887, p. 4.
12. *Ibid.*, January 26, 1905, p. 6.

In 1886, when George was nominated for mayor of New York, most socialists gave him their support. Daniel De Leon, a prominent socialist leader, spoke at the meeting which endorsed his nomination. But a year later, when George ran for secretary of state for New York, the socialists made their support conditional on their principles being included in the election campaign. They declared that the burning social question is not a land tax, but the abolition of all private property in the instruments of production. To this George replied that there could be no place for the socialists in the new party if they pressed their principles. When the convention met at Syracuse, New York, the socialist delegates from New York City did press their principles and were refused seats.

George further infuriated the anarchists, the socialists and other radicals when he refused to condemn the conviction and execution of the Chicago anarchists over the Haymarket affair of May 4, 1886.

Friedrich Engels, a founder along with Karl Marx of the modern communist movement, published a book in 1844 called *The Condition of the Working Class in England.* In a preface to the American edition of 1887 he wrote an evaluation of Henry George:

[I]t seems to me that the Henry George platform, in its present shape, is too narrow to form the basis for anything but a local movement, or at best for a short-lived phase of the general movement. To Henry George, the expropriation of the mass of the people from the land is the great and universal cause of the splitting up of the people into Rich and Poor. Now this is not quite correct historically. In Asiatic and classical antiquity, the predominant form of class oppression was slavery, that is to say, not so much the expropriation of the masses from the land as the appropriation of their persons. . . . In the middle ages, it was not the expropriation of the people *from,* but on the contrary, their appropriation to the land which became the source of feudal oppression. The peasant retained his land, but was attached to it as a serf or villein, and made liable to tribute to the lord in labor and in produce. It was only at the dawn of modern times, toward the end of the fifteenth century, that the expropriation of the peasantry on a large scale laid the foundation for the modern class of wage-workers who possess nothing but their labour-power and can live only by the selling of that labour-power to others. But if the expropriation from the land brought this class into existence, it was the development of capitalist production, of modern industry and agriculture on a large scale, which perpetuated it, increased it, and shaped it into a distinct class with distinct interests and a distinct historical mission. . . . According to Marx, the cause of the present antagonism of the classes and of the social degradation of the working class is their expropriation from *all* means of production, in which the land is of course included.

If Henry George declares land-monopolization to be the sole cause of poverty and misery, he naturally finds the remedy in the resumption of the land by society at large. Now, the Socialists of the school of Marx, too, demand the resumption, by society, of the land, and not only of the land but all other means of production likewise. But even if we leave these out of the question, there is another difference. What is to be done with the land? Modern Socialists, as represented by Marx, demand that it should be held and worked in common and for common account, and the same with all other means of social production, mines, railways, factories, etc.; Henry George would confine himself to letting it out to individuals as at present, merely regulating its distribution and applying the rents for public, instead of, as at present, for private purposes. What the Socialists demand, implies a total revolution of the whole system of social production; what Henry George demands, leaves the present mode of social production untouched, and has, in fact, been anticipated by the extreme section of Ricardian bourgeois economists who, too, demanded the confiscation of the rent of land by the State.[13]

Another socialist comment on George was presented in a letter from George Bernard Shaw to the twenty-fifth anniversary celebration of *Progress and Poverty* referred to in the previous section. Part of Shaw's letter, which was read at the meeting, follows:

When I was thus swept into the great Socialist revival of 1883 I found that five-sixths of those who were swept in with me had been converted by Henry George. This fact would have been far more widely acknowledged had it not been that it was not possible for us to stop where Henry George stopped.

What George did not teach you, you are being taught now by your great trusts and combines, as to which I need only say that if you would take them over as National property as cheerfully as you took the copyrights of all my early books you would find them excellent institutions, quite in the path of progressive evolution, and by no means

---

13. Friedrich Engels, *The Condition of the Working Class in England,* translated and edited by W. O. Henderson and W. H. Chaloner (New York: The Macmillan Company, 1958), pp. 355-356.

to be discouraged or left unregulated as if they were nobody's business but their own.[14]

We have already referred to other writing of Henry George where it related to *Progress and Poverty*. In the following chapter we shall take a closer look at his books and articles after *Progress and Poverty*.

---

14. *The New York Times*, January 25, 1905, p. 6.

CHAPTER 5

Other Writing of Henry George

We have already examined closely George's first and fourth books: *Progress and Poverty;* and *A Perplexed Philosopher,* in which he proclaimed his polemic against Herbert Spencer. In this chapter we shall examine in chronological order by date of publication his three other books and two major articles.[1]

"The Irish Land Question"

George published a pamphlet titled "The Irish Land Question" in 1881 before his first trip to Ireland and England. The title was later changed to "The Land Question," because it applied to other countries as well, and it was republished abroad under the second title.

This work became popular almost at once, and it helped publicize *Progress and Poverty.* It also prepared the way for his visit to Ireland and to his enthusiastic reception there.

Ireland, wrote George, is afflicted with the same atrocious land system "which prevails in all civilized countries." If Ireland were suddenly made a state of the United States, and if American law were substituted for English law there, the Irish landlords would lose nothing, and the tenants would gain nothing. Ireland is a conquered country, but so is every country where landlords have seized the land.

When there is famine among primitive societies, it is because there is not enough food to be had. But during the height of the Irish famine in 1846-47 there was food enough for those who could pay for it. During all the so-called famine, food was being exported from Ireland to

---

1. Some of his very long articles have been classified as books; he therefore wrote five to eight books, depending on what is called a book.

England. So many Irish people were starving not because food was scarce, but because they did not have the means to buy it. It was a financial famine, arising not from the scarcity of food but from the poverty of the people.

We see such hunger on a smaller scale in many countries. The warehouses and shops are full, the rich live in profligate wastefulness, and many men, women and little children are hungry. When men everywhere will cancel the rights of landowners to receive rent from the land, they will be asserting their own natural rights.

George rejected the solution to the problem that some people advocated: that the state should establish peasant proprietorships by buying out the landlords and selling small farms to the tenants on easy terms. This action would not help the mass of farmers because they would still be paying tribute to the landlords through the government. In addition, the trend toward concentrating small farms into large ones would go on in Ireland as it has been going on in Great Britain and the United States. This process of concentration springs from inventions and improvements and economies of large-scale production, which work toward large-scale enterprises in agriculture as well as in industry. "Even butter and cheese are now made and chickens hatched and fattened in factories," George declared.

The fatal defect of schemes such as this one is that it seeks to help only one class of the Irish people—the agricultural tenants. They are not as poor as agricultural and urban laborers; in fact, some Irish tenants are large capitalist farmers of the English type. Selling the tenants the land would leave untouched the fundamental cause of poverty. It would even be politically more difficult to have a 100 percent tax on the rent of land if there were many smallholders instead of a few large landlords.

It is not possible to divide up the land of Ireland to give each family an equal share. "But it is possible to divide the rent equally, or, what amounts to the same thing, to apply it to purposes of common benefit," George stated. To demand the nationalization of the rental income from land would bring the English and Scottish people into the struggle alongside the Irish. It would also unite urban and rural labor and capital against landlordism. "This combination proved its power by winning the battle of free trade in 1846 against the most determined resistance of the landed interest," George asserted.

Social Problems

In 1883 George was asked to write a series of thirteen articles for *Frank Leslie's Illustrated Newspaper.* In the same year he published these articles as his second book, *Social Problems.* Each article became a chapter, and he added eight new chapters and a conclusion.

As a result of writing about "The March of Concentration" in Chapter V, George found himself in a controversy with Francis A. Walker. In addition to all the other accomplishments of this eminent economist, Walker had been chief of the United States Bureau of Statistics and Superintendent of the censuses of 1870 and 1880. The Census Bureau reported that the average size of farms in the United States was declining, from 153 acres in 1870 to 134 acres in 1880. George denied it. He argued that common observation showed that farms were growing larger, that the march toward concentration was proceeding in agriculture as it was in industry. The figures of the censuses themselves denied the Census Bureau's conclusion, said George. Between 1870 and 1880 the number of farms increased 50 percent. But farms under 50 acres were decreasing, while those larger than that were increasing. How, then, could the average size of farms be falling?

In a curt letter to *Frank Leslie's,* Professor Walker suggested that if the census reports were not clear to Mr. George, he could supply "a more elementary statement, illustrated with diagrams" in support of the official statement that the average size of farms was decreasing. George and Walker continued the controversy through the press. The matter was finally cleared up when the Census Bureau explained that the tables for 1870 were based on *improved* area while those for 1880 were based on *total* area. Therefore Walker's comparison of the two censuses was invalid, and George's charge of carelessness was vindicated. The New York *Sun,* in summarizing the long controversy in which Walker had been rather contemptuous of George, wrote:

It is amusing because, while there is no lack of suavity and decorum on the part of Mr. George, his opponent squirms and sputters as one flagrant blunder after another is brought forward and the spike of logic is driven home through his egregious fallacies.[2]

2. Henry George, Jr., *The Life of Henry George* (New York: Robert Schalkenbach Foundation, 1960), p. 409. [Originally published in 1900.]

Is there not enough wealth to go around for all, asked George, if it were distributed properly? And could we not produce much more than we do? Wherever we look we see the most stupendous waste of productive forces. The masses of people are overcrowded in city tenement-houses while vacant lots are plentiful. Settlers go to Montana, Dakota and Manitoba while land much nearer to the centers of population remains untilled. Much of our machinery is idle, people are unemployed, and output is restricted while many people suffer want. It took the waste and destruction of the civil war to bring prosperity to the United States. George went on to say:

The masses of the people lived better, dressed better, found it easier to get a living, and had more luxuries and amusements than in normal times. There was more real, tangible wealth in the North at the close than at the beginning of the war. Nor was it the great issue of paper money, nor the creation of the debt, which caused this prosperity. The government presses struck off promises to pay; they could not print ships, cannon, arms, tools, food and clothing. Nor did we borrow these things from other countries or "from posterity." Our bonds did not begin to go to Europe until the close of the war, and the people of one generation can no more borrow from the people of a subsequent generation than we who live on this planet can borrow from the inhabitants of another planet or another solar system. The wealth consumed and destroyed by our fleets and armies came from the then existing stock of wealth. We could have carried on the war without the issue of a single bond, if, when we did not shrink from taking from wife and children their only bread-winner, we had not shrunk from taking the wealth of the rich.

Our armies and fleets were maintained, the enormous unproductive and destructive use of wealth was kept up, by the labor and capital then and there engaged in production. And it was that the demand caused by the war stimulated productive forces into activity that the enormous drain of the war was not only supplied, but that the North grew richer. The waste of labor in marching and countermarching, in digging trenches, throwing up earthworks, and fighting battles, the waste of wealth consumed or destroyed by our armies and fleets, did not amount to as much as the waste constantly going on from unemployed labor and idle or partially used machinery.

It is evident that this enormous waste of productive power is due, not to defects in the laws of nature, but to social maladjustments which deny to labor access to the natural opportunities of labor and rob the laborer of his just reward.[3]

3. Henry George, *Social Problems* (New York: Robert Schalkenbach Foundation, 1966), pp. 75-76. [Originally published in 1883.]

George's powerful descriptions of the poverty that shocked him appeared in this book also:

In New York, as I write, the newspapers and the churches are calling for subscriptions to their "fresh-air funds," that little children may be taken for a day or for a week from the deadly heat of stifling tenement rooms and given a breath of the fresh breeze of sea-shore or mountain; but how little does it avail, when we take such children only to return them to their previous conditions—conditions which to many mean even worse than death of the body; conditions which make it certain that of the lives that may thus be saved, some are saved for the brothel and the almshouse, and some for the penitentiary. We may go on forever merely raising fresh-air funds, and how great soever be the funds we raise, the need will only grow, and children—just such children as those of whom Christ said, "Take heed that ye despise not one of these little ones; for I say unto you, that in heaven their angels do always behold the face of my Father"—will die like flies, so long as poverty compels fathers and mothers to the life of the squalid tenement room. We may open "midnight missions" and support "Christian homes for destitute young girls," but what will they avail in the face of general conditions which render so many men unable to support a wife; which make young girls think it a privilege to be permitted to earn three dollars by eighty-one hours' work, and which can drive a mother to such despair that she will throw her babies from a wharf of our Christian city and then leap into the river herself! How vainly shall we endeavor to repress crime by our barbarous punishment of the poorer class of criminals as long as children are reared in the brutalizing influences of poverty, so long as the bite of want drives men to crime! How little better than idle is it for us to prohibit infant labor in factories when the scale of wages is so low that it will not enable fathers to support their families without the earnings of their little children! How shall we try to prevent political corruption by framing new checks and setting one official to watch another official, when the fear of want stimulates the lust for wealth, and the rich thief is honored while honest poverty is despised?. . .

An English writer has divided all men into three classes—workers, beggars and thieves. The classification is not complimentary to the "upper classes" and the "better classes," as they are accustomed to esteem themselves, yet it is economically true. There are only three ways by which any individual can get wealth—by work, by gift or by theft. And, clearly, the reason why the workers get so little is that the beggars and thieves get so much. When a man gets wealth that he does not produce, he necessarily gets it at the expense of those who produce it.[4]

---

4. *Ibid.*, pp. 81-82, 84.

George argued that access to the land would solve the labor problem, eliminate poverty and unemployment, and rectify the extreme inequities in the distribution of income:

The possibility of indefinite expansion in the primary occupations, the ability of every one to make a living by resort to them, would produce elasticity throughout the whole industrial system.

Under such conditions capital could not oppress labor. At present, in any dispute between capital and labor, capital enjoys the enormous advantage of being better able to wait. Capital wastes when not employed; but labor starves. Where, however, labor could always employ itself, the disadvantage in any conflict would be on the side of capital, while that surplus of unemployed labor which enables capital to make such advantageous bargains with labor would not exist. The man who wanted to get others to work for him would not find men crowding for employment, but, finding all labor already employed, would have to offer higher wages, in order to tempt them into his employment, than the men he wanted could make for themselves. The competition would be that of employers to obtain workmen, rather than that of workmen to get employment, and thus the advantages which the accumulation of capital gives in the production of wealth would (save enough to secure the accumulation and employment of capital) go ultimately to labor. In such a state of things, instead of thinking that the man who employed another was doing him a favor, we would rather look upon the man who went to work for another as the obliging party. . . .

But it may be said, as I have often heard it said, "We do not all want land! We cannot all become farmers!"

To this I reply that we *do* all want land, though it may be in different ways and in varying degrees. Without land no human being can live; without land no human occupation can be carried on. Agriculture is not the only use of land. It is only one of many. And just as the uppermost story of the tallest building rests upon land as truly as the lowest, so is the operative as truly a user of land as is the farmer. As all wealth is in the last analysis the resultant of land and labor, so is all production in the last analysis the expenditure of labor upon land.

Nor is it true that we could not all become farmers. That *is* the one thing that we might all become. If all men were merchants, or tailors, or mechanics, all men would soon starve. But there have been, and still exist, societies in which all get their living directly from nature. The occupations that resort directly to nature are the primitive occupations, from which, as society progresses, all others are differentiated. No matter how complex the industrial organization, these must always remain the fundamental occupations, upon which all other occupations rest, just as the upper stories of a building rest upon the foundation.

Now, as ever, "the farmer feedeth all." And necessarily, the condition of labor in these first and widest of occupations, determines the general condition of labor, just as the level of the ocean determines the level of all its arms and bays and seas. Where there is a great demand for labor in agriculture, and wages are high, there must soon be a great demand for labor, and high wages, in all occupations. Where it is difficult to get employment in agriculture, and wages are low, there must soon be a difficulty of obtaining employment, and low wages, in all occupations. Now, what determines the demand for labor and the rate of wages in agriculture is manifestly the ability of labor to employ itself—that is to say, the ease with which land can be obtained. This is the reason that in new countries, where land is easily had, wages, not merely in agriculture, but in all occupations, are higher than in older countries, where land is hard to get. And thus it is that, as the value of land increases, wages fall, and the difficulty in finding employment arises.[5]

Protection or Free Trade

In 1883, when George was working on *Protection or Free Trade,* he lost his manuscript. When he was preparing to move from a house on Fourteenth Street in Manhattan to another on Hancock Street in Brooklyn, he asked a servant to carry off and destroy an accumulation of waste papers. He inadvertently included his manuscript of about one hundred pages. George completed this book, his third, and had it published in 1886. Tom L. Johnson and others helped distribute this book so that its circulation reached two million copies in less than eight years.

George's subtitle to the book showed the focus of his thinking. It was "An Examination of the Tariff Question, with Especial Regard to the Interests of Labor." He considered the tariff issue as part of larger social questions: the role of government, the question of taxes, and the measures required to promote the well-being of all mankind.

Public policy must be concerned with raising and maintaining wage rates, he argued. The question of wages is important not only to laborers, but to society as a whole, for high wages promote prosperity:

---

5. *Ibid.,* pp. 134-137.

I accept as good and praiseworthy the ends avowed by the advocates of protective tariffs. What I propose to inquire is whether protective tariffs are in reality conducive to these ends.[6]

Workingmen, said George, know they are underpaid. In seeking to protect themselves against competition, they favor protective tariffs. Protectionists at least profess concern for workers and proclaim their desire to use the powers of government to raise and maintain wages. Most free traders, in contrast, show no concern for workers; they do not care to see wage rates rise, and they want the government to do nothing in that direction. They proclaim "supply and demand to be the only true and rightful regulator of the price of labor as of the price of pig-iron." They protest against restrictions on the production of wealth, but they ignore the monstrous injustice of its distribution.

George was convinced of an international harmony of interests that could be served best through free trade. He wrote:

Religion and experience alike teach us that the highest good of each is to be sought in the good of others; that the true interests of men are harmonious, not antagonistic; that prosperity is the daughter of good will and peace; and that want and destruction follow enmity and strife. The protective theory, on the other hand, implies the opposition of national interests; that the gain of one people is the loss of others; that each must seek its own good by constant efforts to get advantage over others and to prevent others from getting advantage over it. It makes of nations rivals instead of cooperators; it inculcates a warfare of restrictions and prohibitions and searchings and seizures, which differs in weapons, but not in spirit, from that warfare which sinks ships and burns cities. Can we imagine the nations beating their swords into plowshares and their spears into pruning hooks and yet maintaining hostile tariffs?[7]

All improvements in transportation, all labor-saving inventions and discoveries, are antagonistic to protection. We maintain a tariff for the avowed purpose of keeping out the products of cheap foreign labor; yet machines are being invented that produce goods cheaper than the cheapest foreign labor. China is consistently protectionist by not only

---

6. Henry George, *Protection or Free Trade* (New York: Robert Schalkenbach Foundation, 1966), p. 5 [Originally published in 1886.]
7. *Ibid.*, p. 31.

prohibiting foreign commerce but also by forbidding the introduction of labor-saving machinery.

Even if tariffs are not protective, they are used frequently for raising revenue. These are indirect taxes. They are expensive to collect, and they give rise to bribery and corruption. But even worse, when such taxation is imposed on articles of general use, it bears much more heavily on the poor than on the rich, says George:

Since such taxation falls on people not according to what they have, but according to what they consume, it is heaviest on those whose consumption is largest in proportion to their means. As much sugar is needed to sweeten a cup of tea for a working-girl as for the richest lady in the land, but the proportion of their means which a tax on sugar compels each to contribute to the government is in the case of the one much greater than in the case of the other. So it is with all taxes that increase the cost of articles of general consumption. They bear far more heavily on married men than on bachelors; on those who have children than on those who have none; on those barely able to support their families than on those whose incomes leave them a large surplus. . . .

Even if cheaper articles were taxed at no higher rates than the more costly, such taxation would be grossly unjust; but in indirect taxation there is always a tendency to impose heavier taxes on the cheaper articles used by all than on the more costly articles used only by the rich. This arises from the necessities of the case. Not only do the larger amounts of articles of common consumption afford a wider base for large revenues than the smaller amounts of more costly articles, but taxes imposed on them cannot be so easily evaded. For instance, while articles in use by the poor as well as the rich are under our tariff taxed fifty and a hundred, and even a hundred and fifty per cent: the tax on diamonds is only ten per cent. . . .

That indirect taxes thus bear far more heavily on the poor than on the rich is undoubtedly one of the reasons why they have so readily been adopted. The rich are ever the powerful, and under all forms of government have most influence in forming public opinion and framing laws, while the poor are ever the voiceless.[8]

Protective tariffs are advocated to encourage home industry. This can be done by protecting established old industries, or by encouraging the establishment of new industries—the infant industry argument. Certainly the protectionists of Europe wish to increase the profits of

8. *Ibid.*, pp. 71-73.

old, established industries. But in the United States the infant industry argument has been used widely to justify tariffs, even as far back as 1791 in Alexander Hamilton's "Report on Manufactures." The objections to this defense of tariffs are: first, we don't know which industries to encourage; second, the strongest industries and their least scrupulous leaders will be most influential and successful in getting government benefits, while the weak will fall farther behind; third, if an industry relies on government protection it will not develop independent strength and initiative.

If the aim of the protectionists is to diminish imports, what is their attitude toward exports? Here is how George answered this question:

The aim of protection is to diminish imports, never to diminish exports. On the contrary, the protectionist habit is to regard exports with favor, and to consider the country which exports most and imports least as doing the most profitable trade. When exports exceed imports there is said to be a favorable balance of trade. When imports exceed exports there is said to be an unfavorable balance of trade. In accordance with this idea all protectionist countries afford every facility for sending things away and fine men for bringing things in.

If the things which we thus try to send away and prevent coming in were pests and vermin—things of which all men want as little as possible—this policy would conform to reason. But the things of which exports and imports consist are not things that nature forces on us against our will, and that we have to struggle to rid ourselves of; but things that nature gives only in return for labor, things for which men make exertions and undergo privations. Him who has or can command much of these things we call rich; him who has little we call poor; and when we say that a country increases in wealth we mean that the amount of these things which it contains increases faster than its population. What, then, is more repugnant to reason than the notion that the way to increase the wealth of a country is to promote the sending of such things away and to prevent the bringing of them in? Could there be a queerer inversion of ideas? Should we not think even a dog had lost his senses that snapped and snarled when given a bone, and wagged his tail when a bone was taken from him?

Lawyers may profit by quarrels, doctors by diseases, rat-catchers by the prevalence of vermin, and so it may be to the interest of some of the individuals of a nation to have as much as possible of the good things which we call "goods" sent away, and as little as possible brought in. But protectionists claim that it is for the benefit of a community, as a whole, of a nation considered as one man, to make it easy to send goods away and difficult to bring them in.[9]

   George also pointed out that exports and imports, so far as they are induced by trade, rise and fall together. To impose any restrictions on one is necessarily to lessen the other. But some exports are induced, not by trade, but by the drain of wealth for which no return is made. For example, France had a surplus of exports to Germany in 1871 because of the tribute she owed after losing the war. The foreign debt fastened upon Egypt by Great Britain in the nineteenth century resulted in her exporting more than she imported. Ireland exported farm produce to pay rent to absentee landlords. These examples show that exporting may be more detrimental than importing.

   George understood David Ricardo's law of comparative advantage as providing the basis for free trade. He imagined a situation in which one country is more efficient than another in producing everything. With free trade between them, it would be impossible for the more efficient country to export without importing. The people of the more efficient country would import those products in which their margin of efficiency was smallest; they would export those goods in which their margin of efficiency was greatest. "By this exchange both peoples would gain," George concluded.

   After presenting a strong case against tariffs, George emphasized the inadequacy of the free-trade argument. There is a *tendency*, he said, for free trade to increase the production of wealth, thereby *permitting* the increase of wages. But from this it does not follow that free trade would be of any benefit to the working class. The effect of the repeal of tariffs would be similar to that of the inventions and discoveries which increase the production of wealth. In either case, the benefits of increased efficiency go to the owners of the land. In Great Britain free trade after 1846 did not abolish hunger or improve the lot of labor because landlords continued to exact their toll. Along with free trade, we need the single tax on land.

"An Open Letter to Pope Leo XIII"

   In 1891 Pope Leo XIII issued an Encyclical Letter on the Condition of Labor *(Rerum Novarum)*. George thought it was aimed at the single

9. *Ibid.,* pp. 112-113.

tax movement, and some high Church officials in the United States and England gleefully agreed with him on that score. George published a reply in the same year called "The Condition of Labor. An Open Letter to Pope Leo XIII." It was 25,000 words long, more than twice the length of the Pope's Encyclical. It was a well-written document, and George's friends, concerned about his health, took it as evidence that he had recovered completely from his stroke of the year before.

The Encyclical Letter appeared at a time when social questions were being considered by secular rather than Church groups. More and more people were drifting away from the Church. Although *Rerum Novarum* reasserted the right of private property against the encroachments of the state, Pope Leo went on to say that the state is within its rights in seeking to prevent the exploitation of labor. Workers should receive their just reward, and legislation, trade unions and cooperative organizations were all legitimate means to achieve this goal. The Encyclical Letter stimulated the formation of Catholic trade unions and the Catholic social movement. This reduced the tendency of workers to leave the Church, and even ruling circles welcomed this approach as an alternative to Marxist ideology among the disaffected.

Pope Leo warned of the growing conflicts in social relations arising from the growth of industry, the discoveries of science, the rise of great fortunes of individuals and the poverty of the masses, the combinations of working people, and finally a general moral deterioration: "And the danger lies in this, that crafty agitators constantly make use of these disputes to pervert men's judgments and to stir up the people to sedition."[10]

Remedies must be found—quickly—for the misery and wretchedness which press so heavily on the very poor. The poor are being victimized by the rich, and the socialists are taking advantage of the situation by trying to eliminate private property in favor of common property. Such a proposal is unjust and against the interests of the workers themselves. Private ownership, including that of land, is in accordance with nature's law, declared Pope Leo.

---

10. Henry George, *The Condition of Labor. An Open Letter to Pope Leo XIII*, with an *Appendix. Encyclical Letter of Pope Leo XIII on the Condition of Labor* (New York: Robert Schalkenbach Foundation, 1965), p. 110. [Originally published in 1891.]

These arguments are so strong and convincing that it seems surprising that certain obsolete opinions should now be revived in opposition to what is here laid down. We are told that it is right for private persons to have the use of the soil and the fruits of their land, but that it is unjust for any one to possess as owner either the land on which he has built or the estate which he has cultivated. But those who assert this do not perceive that they are robbing man of what his own labor has produced. For the soil which is tilled and cultivated with toil and skill utterly changes its condition; it was wild before, it is now fruitful; it was barren, and now it brings forth in abundance. That which has thus altered and improved it becomes so truly part of itself as to be in great measure indistinguishable and inseparable from it. Is it just that the fruit of a man's sweat and labor should be enjoyed by another? As effects follow their cause, so it is just and right that the results of labor should belong to him who has labored.[11]

Pope Leo had denounced the idea of hostility between classes. It is irrational and false to believe that rich and poor are intended by nature to live at war with one another, he wrote:

Each requires the other; capital cannot do without labor, nor labor without capital. Mutual agreement results in pleasantness and good order; perpetual conflict necessarily produces confusion and outrage. Now, in preventing such strife as this, and in making it impossible, the efficacy of Christianity is marvelous and manifold. First of all, there is nothing more powerful than Religion (of which the Church is the interpreter and guardian) in drawing rich and poor together, by reminding each class of its duties to the other, and especially of the duties of justice. Thus Religion teaches the laboring-man and the workman to carry out honestly and well all equitable agreements freely made; never to injure capital, or to outrage the person of an employer; never to employ violence in representing his own cause, or to engage in riot or disorder; and to have nothing to do with men of evil principles, who work upon the people with artful promises, and raise foolish hopes which usually end in disaster and in repentance when too late. Religion teaches the rich man and the employer that their work-people are not their slaves; that they must respect in every man his dignity as a man and as a Christian; that labor is nothing to be ashamed of, if we listen to right reason and to Christian philosophy, but is an honorable employment, enabling a man to sustain his life in an upright and creditable way; and that it is shameful and inhuman to treat men like chattels to make money by, or to look upon them merely as so much

11. *Ibid.*, pp. 114-115.

muscle or physical power. . . . Then, again, the employer must never tax his work-people beyond their strength, nor employ them in work unsuited to their sex or age. His great and principal obligation is to give to every one that which is just. . . .

Were these prospects carefully obeyed and followed, would not strife die out and cease?

But the Church, with Jesus Christ for its Master and Guide, aims higher still. It lays down precepts yet more perfect, and tries to bind class to class in friendliness and good understanding.[12]

Writing at a time when the laissez-faire view was predominant, Leo urged a significant role for government in ameliorating social conditions:

Let us now, therefore, inquire what part the State should play in the work of remedy and relief. . . .

The first duty, therefore, of the rulers of the State should be to make sure that the laws and institutions, the general character and administration of the commonwealth, shall be such as to produce of themselves public well-being and private prosperity. This is the proper office of wise statesmanship and the work of the heads of the State. . . . Here, then, it is in the power of a ruler to benefit every order of the State, and amongst the rest to promote in the highest degree the interests of the poor; and this by virtue of his office, and without being exposed to any suspicion of undue interference—for it is the province of the commonwealth to consult for the common good. And the more that is done for the working population by the general laws of the country, the less need will there be to seek for particular means to relieve them.

There is another and a deeper consideration which must not be lost sight of. To the State the interests of all are equal, whether high or low. The poor are members of the national community equally with the rich; they are real component parts, living parts, which make up, through the family, the living body; and it need hardly be said that they are by far the majority. It would be irrational to neglect one portion of the citizens and to favor another; and therefore the public administration must duly and solicitously provide for the welfare and the comfort of the working-people, or else that law of justice will be violated which ordains that each shall have his due. . . .

[I] t is only by the labor of the working-man that States grow rich. Justice, therefore, demands that the interests of the poorer population be carefully watched over by the Administration, so that they who

12. *Ibid.*, pp. 120-122.

contribute so largely to the advantage of the community may themselves share in the benefits they create—that being housed, clothed, and enabled to support life, they may find their existence less hard and more endurable. . . .

Whenever the general interest of any particular class suffers, or is threatened with, evils which can in no other way be met, the public authority must step in to meet them. . . .

Rights must be religiously respected wherever they are found; and it is the duty of the public authority to prevent and punish injury, and to protect each one in the possession of his own. Still, when there is question of protecting the rights of individuals, the poor and helpless have a claim to special consideration. The richer population have many ways of protecting themselves, and stand less in need of help from the State; those who are badly off have no resources of their own to fall back upon, and must chiefly rely upon the assistance of the State. And it is for this reason that wage-earners, who are undoubtedly among the weak and necessitous, should be specially cared for and protected by the commonwealth.[13]

Leo criticized excessive hours of work, child labor, and the mistreatment of women by employing them at certain trades for which they were not suited. As a rule workers and employers should arrive freely at wage agreements. But the dictate of nature is that the remuneration must be enough to support the worker in reasonable and frugal comfort. If a worker accepts less than this, he is the victim of force and injustice. If we are to avoid undue interference by the state, then the state should approve of workers' own organizations that protect their interests. These include cooperative organizations and unions, which should be based firmly on religious principles, he declared:

Let our associations, then, look first and before all to God; let religious instruction have therein a foremost place, each one being carefully taught what is his duty to God, what to believe, what to hope for, and how to work out his salvation; and let all be warned and fortified with especial solicitude against wrong opinions and false teaching. . . .

The rights and duties of employers should be the subject of careful consideration as compared with the rights and duties of the employed. If it should happen that either a master or a workman deemed himself injured, nothing would be more desirable than that there should be a

---

13. *Ibid.,* pp. 129-134.

committee composed of honest and capable men of the Association itself, whose duty it should be, by the laws of the Assocation, to decide the dispute. Among the purposes of a Society should be to try to arrange for a continuous supply of work at all times and seasons; and to create a fund from which the members may be helped in their necessities, not only in cases of accident, but also in sickness, old age, and misfortune.[14]

George, in his reply to Pope Leo XIII, stated that the Encyclical Letter condemned his own single tax views which deserved the Church's support. He therefore was presenting his case to the Pope, and he opened his presentation with a defense of the tax on rent on religious grounds: "God has intended the state to obtain the revenues it needs by the taxation of land values." He denied that God is a bungler who is constantly bringing more people into His world than He has made provision for. Poverty amid wealth and seething discontent are the inevitable results of our ignoring God's intent.

George chided Leo for his broad, blanket defense of private property; property based on violence and robbery, said the American, cannot be defended. Property in slaves is an example, and property in land is another. "[Y]ou give us equal rights in heaven, but deny us equal rights on earth! . . . [Y]our Encyclical gives the gospel to the laborers and the earth to the landlords."

In addition to the ethical-religious side of his argument, George presented the economic side, with which we are already familiar.

By implication Leo had condemned the single taxers along with those radicals who opposed private property in all means of production. George disassociated himself and his movement from the socialists:

We differ from the socialists in our diagnosis of the evil and we differ from them as to remedies. We have no fear of capital, regarding it as the natural handmaiden of labor; we look on interest in itself as natural and just; we would set no limit to accumulation, nor impose on the rich any burden that is not equally placed on the poor; we see no evil in competition, but deem unrestricted competition to be as necessary to the health of the industrial and social organism as the free circulation of the blood is to the health of the bodily organism—to be the agency whereby the fullest cooperation is to be secured. We would simply take

---

14. *Ibid.*, pp. 147-148.

for the community what belongs to the community, the value that attaches to land by the growth of the community; leave sacredly to the individual all that belongs to the individual; and, treating necessary monopolies as functions of the state, abolish all restrictions and prohibitions save those required for public health, safety, morals and convenience.

But the fundamental difference—the difference I ask your Holiness specially to note, is in this: socialism in all its phases looks on the evils of our civilization as springing from the inadequacy or inharmony of natural relations, which must be artificially organized or improved. In its idea there devolves on the state the necessity of intelligently organizing the industrial relations of men; the construction, as it were, of a great machine whose complicated parts shall properly work together under the direction of human intelligence. This is the reason why socialism tends toward atheism. Failing to see the order and symmetry of natural law, it fails to recognize God.

On the other hand, we who call ourselves single-tax men (a name which expresses merely our practical propositions) see in the social and industrial relations of men not a machine which requires construction, but an organism which needs only to be suffered to grow. We see in the natural social and industrial laws such harmony as we see in the adjustments of the human body, and that as far transcends the power of man's intelligence to order and direct as it is beyond man's intelligence to order and direct the vital movements of his frame. We see in these social and industrial laws so close a relation to the moral law as must spring from the same Authorship, and that proves the moral law to be the sure guide of man where his intelligence would wander and go astray. Thus, to us, all that is needed to remedy the evils of our time is to do justice and give freedom. This is the reason why our beliefs tend toward, nay are indeed the only beliefs consistent with a firm and reverent faith in God, and with the recognition of his law as the supreme law which men must follow if they would secure prosperity and avoid destruction.[15]

A copy of George's letter, printed in Italian and handsomely bound, was presented to Pope Leo XIII, although he never acknowledged its receipt. The Church did modify its opposition to the single tax, and it was believed that George was influential in promoting this change in attitude.

---

15. *Ibid.,* pp. 61-62.

The Science of Political Economy

In 1891 George began writing what he intended to be a short textbook on political economy. This work grew in size and scope, but it remained unfinished when he died in 1897. Except for minor editing by his son, Henry George, Jr., the book was published in the following year as he left it, a work of 528 pages.

In *The Science of Political Economy* George summarized his economic and philosophical views. He criticized other economists, probed the history of economic doctrines, reviewed *Progress and Poverty* and its reception by the public, and presented some autobiographical material. He attempted to cover and integrate the whole field of political economy.

All large political questions, said George in his introduction, are at bottom economic questions. Under present social conditions there is something wrong with the distribution of wealth; but political economy and its professors have been dominated by the wealthy, who wish to obscure the truth.

What is the origin and genesis of civilizations? One of the most striking differences between man and the lower animals is that man is the unsatisfied animal. A more fundamental difference is that man is endowed with the quality of reason. He has what animals lack—the power of tracing effect to cause, and from cause to reason out the effect. This power of "thinking things out," the power of tracing causal relations, the power of reason, makes man a superior creature. He is the only producer among all the animals in the true sense of the term. The same quality of reason that results in his being a producer also makes him, whenever exchange becomes possible, an exchanger. Civilization begins with exchange or trade, George said.

The animals do not develop civilization, because they do not trade. . . . We are accustomed to speak of certain peoples as uncivilized, and of certain other peoples as civilized or fully civilized, but in truth such use of terms is merely relative. To find an utterly uncivilized people we must find a people among whom there is no exchange or trade. Such a people does not exist, and, so far as our knowledge goes, never did. To find a fully civilized people we must find a people among whom exchange or trade is absolutely free, and has reached the fullest development to which human desires can carry it. There is, as yet, unfortunately, no such people.[16]

Science, said, George, literally means knowledge. Science does not include all knowledge, but only knowledge related to the laws of nature. The object of even the social sciences is to discover the laws of nature in which human laws, customs and modes of thought originate.

If political economy is a science—and if not it is hardly worth the while of earnest men to bother themselves with it—it must follow the rules of science, and seek in natural law the causes of the phenomena which it investigates. With human law, except as furnishing illustrations and supplying subjects for its investigation, it has, as I have already said, nothing whatever to do. It is concerned with the permanent, not with the transient; with the laws of nature, not with the laws of man.[17]

George looked into the origins of his own doctrine, some of which he was unaware of when he wrote *Progress and Poverty*. Foremost among the early advocates of a tax on rent was François Quesnay, physician to King Louis XV of France and leader of the French physiocratic school. These men, said George, saw that there is but one source from which men can draw for all their material needs—land; and that there is but one means by which land can be made to produce—labor. All real wealth therefore comes from the application of labor to the land. Quesnay and his followers understood that land produced a surplus or net product after all other expenses of production are met; this is what we call rent. They advocated a single tax, a tax only on economic rent, the unearned increment that comes from land wherever society progresses. The physiocrats erred, however, in thinking that only agriculture is productive. Urban rents, said George, should also be taxed, and not only agricultural rents, in which the physiocrats also included fisheries and mines.

George wrote that he had never heard of the physiocrats until after he published "Our Land and Land Policy" in 1871.

Thomas Spence delivered a lecture before the Philosophical Society of Newcastle, England, in 1775; this was a year before the publication

16. Henry George, *The Science of Political Economy* (New York: Robert Schalkenbach Foundation, 1968), pp. 36-37. [Originally published in 1898.]
17. *Ibid.*, p. 64.

of Adam Smith's *Wealth of Nations.* The Society, said Spence, did him the honor of expelling him because of his lecture. He had declared that all men "have as equal and just a property in land as they have in liberty, air, or the light and heat of the sun." He proposed that the value of land should be taken for all public expenses, and all other taxes should be abolished.

William Ogilvie, Professor of Humanities in King's College, Aberdeen, Scotland, published a book in 1782 in which he declared that land is a birthright which every citizen still retains. He advocated the taxation of land with the abolition of all other taxes.

In 1850 the Scotsman Patrick Edward Dove published a book in which he advocated free trade and the single tax. His book drew no attention either in Great Britain or the United States, and George never heard of it until after the publication of *Progress and Poverty.* In fact George was once accused of plagiarizing from Dove. He would have ignored the charge except that it had been noted extensively in the press and elsewhere. George pointed out that if similarity of thought and priority of authorship on Dove's part proved George a plagiarist, then the same reasoning would prove Dove to have copied from Herbert Spencer, who wrote similarly and earlier; it would likewise prove that Spencer stole from Ogilvie, and Ogilvie from Spence. George said that as he heard of more and more of his predecessors who had the same ideas as he had arrived at independently, that gave additional evidence that they were all on the true track.

George challenged the law of diminishing returns in greater detail than he had in *Progress and Poverty.* This alleged law, he said, is considered to be important because it relates to the law of rent and it seems to give support to the Malthusian doctrine that population tends to outrun subsistence. This law denies the justice of the Creator and assumes that He is constantly doing what any mere human host would be ashamed to do: bringing more guests to the table than can be fed, declared George. He added:

This law of diminishing returns in agriculture it is further explained applies also to mining, and in short to all the primary or extractive industries, which give the character of wealth to what was not before wealth, but not to those secondary or subsequent industries which add an additional increase of wealth to what was already wealth. Thus since the law of diminishing productiveness in agriculture does not apply to the secondary industries, it is assumed that any increased application of labor (and capital) in manufacturing for instance, would continue to yield a proportionate and more than proportionate return. And as conclusive and axiomatic proof of this law of diminishing productiveness in agriculture, it is said that were it not for this peculiar law, and were it, on the contrary (as it is assumed it would be without it), the fact that additional application of labor would result in a proportionately increased production from the same land, one single farm would suffice to raise all the agricultural produce required to feed the whole population of England, of the United States or any other country, or of course, of the whole world, by mere increase in the application of labor.

This proposition seems to have been generally accepted by professional economists as a valid *reductio ad absurdum.*[18]

This so-called law of diminishing returns, said George, applies to industry as well as agriculture. It derives from the truth that a certain amount of space is required for both agricultural and industrial activities. In any occupation the crowding of more and more labor in a limited space must result first in a proportionate lessening of the product, and finally in an absolute decline. This alleged law of diminishing returns in agriculture is really the special law of material existence. It applies to making bricks as fully as to growing beets, he declared:

A single man engaged in making a thousand bricks would greatly waste labor if he were to diffuse his exertions over a square mile or a square acre, digging and burning the clay for one brick here, and for another some distance apart. His exertion would yield a much larger return if more closely concentrated in space. But there is a point in this concentration in space where the increase of exertion will begin to diminish its proportionate yield. In the same superficial area required for the production of one brick, two bricks may be produced to advantage. But this concentration of labor in space cannot be continued indefinitely without diminishing the return and finally bringing production to a stop. To get the clay for a thousand bricks without use of more surface of the earth than is required to get the clay for one brick, would involve, even if it were possible at all, an enormous loss in the productiveness of the labor. And so if an attempt were made to put

18. *Ibid.,* p. 337.

a thousand men to work in making brick on an area in which two men might work with advantage, the result would be not merely that the exertion of the thousand men could not produce five hundred times as much as the exertion of two men, but that it would produce nothing at all. Men so crowded would prevent each other from working.[19]

In view of our criticism of George on the law of diminishing returns presented in Chapter 3 above, the following must be said: he was absolutely correct in contending that the principle applies to industry as well as to agriculture. This was not appreciated in his time, and he was ahead of his contemporary orthodox economists in emphasizing this point. But instead of disproving this law, he showed it to be generally applicable in all spheres of production.

---

19. *Ibid.*, pp. 360-361.

CHAPTER 6

The Life of Henry George After Progress and Poverty

George had 18 years of life left after *Progress and Poverty* was completed. They were years of struggle and self-sacrifice, of intense activity, of world fame, of a crusade he never lost faith in.

George's Speaking Tours Abroad

In October, 1881, George sailed to the United Kingdom with his wife and two daughters. He had been engaged for a three months' speaking tour by the newspaper *Irish World,* which was published in New York City. He remained there for a year, returning to New York in October 1882 "pretty near famous."

At this time 500 Irish men and women were incarcerated as political prisioners, including Charles Parnell and two other members of Parliament. George noted that Ireland was a country of only 32,000 square miles (which is smaller than Indiana and only slightly larger than Maine), and with a population of little more than five million. Yet in time of peace if required 15,000 military constables and 40,000 picked troops to govern the country. George denounced British rule in Ireland and the oppressive system of land tenure that robbed the people. Miss Helen Taylor, stepdaughter of John Stuart Mill, became a close friend of the Georges; she too was very much involved in the Irish struggles for land and freedom.

In western Ireland George was arrested as a "suspicious stranger" along with his companion, a master of Eton College. Their luggage was searched and their papers read; after three hours they were released. In a nearby town in the same police district, George noticed that there was but one hand pump to supply water to the entire village, and no doctor, but there were twenty-six police constables and fifty-six soldiers. The next day George was again arrested, but his companion was not. He was taken before the same magistrate who had released him the day before. That official justified the arrest and then discharged George again.

George and his wife became involved with Michael Davitt, the great Irish rebel leader, during their visit to Ireland and England. Davitt was the son of a peasant farmer who had been evicted in 1852 for nonpayment of rent. Michael was at work in a cotton mill at ten years of age, and at eleven he lost his right arm in an industrial accident. He was then sent to school, and at fifteen he became a newsboy and printer's "devil." In 1870, as a young man of twenty-four, he was arrested for sending firearms into Ireland and sentenced to fifteen years of penal servitude. He was released after serving seven years. Linking the campaign for Irish independence with the nationalization of land, Davitt helped found the Land League in 1879. He was rearrested, released in 1882, and again imprisoned for three months in 1883. He had been elected to Parliament in 1882 but was disqualified because he had been a convict. In 1892 he was elected again but was unseated by petition. After being elected a third time, he had to vacate his seat because of his bankruptcy due to the expenses of previous litigation. In 1895 he was elected to Parliament for the fourth time, and served until he resigned his seat in protest over the Boer War. He died in 1906 in Dublin at 60 years of age, an embittered nationalist, anti-English, anti-clerical, and skeptical of the value of purely parliamentary agitation for Home Rule.

George met Davitt in New York City in the fall of 1880 when the latter had arrived on Land League business. Davitt pledged that his organization would push *Progress and Poverty* in Great Britain.

When the English government suppressed the Land League, the Ladies' Land League was organized to carry on the agitation. While Henry George was in London and his wife and daughters were in Dublin, the secret leaked out from government circles that the Ladies' Land League was about to be proscribed and its leaders arrested. Two of the leaders fled immediately to London after one of them sent her official records of the organization to Annie George for safekeeping. The remaining women invited Mrs. George to preside that day over the regular business meeting of the Ladies' Land League. She had never before presided over a meeting, and her nervousness was heightened by the presence of men who turned out to be government detectives and correspondents for various publications. But the appearance of an American woman in the chair disconcerted the government officials, and they did not proscribe the League.

When Michael Davitt was released from prison, George hurried from Dublin to London to see him; their meeting lasted late into the night. That same evening of May 6, 1882, the new Chief Secretary and Under Secretary arrived in Dublin and were stabbed to death in Phoenix Park. George was awakened early in the morning with a telegram from a friend in Dublin telling him of the assassinations. George hurried to Davitt's hotel to wake him and tell him the grim news. "My God!" Davitt exclaimed, "have I got out of Portland [prison] for this!" And then he added mournfully, "For the first time in my life I despair. It seems like the curse that has always followed Ireland."

There were fears that the English would rise in violent retaliation against the Irish residents in their midst. Some advised that the Irish leaders should seek safety in France. This was the sentiment at a dinner party Henry and Annie George attended that Sunday night. When he raised the question as to what Davitt should do, she was alone in saying that he "should go to Ireland by the first train, and be a leader to the people in this hour of dismay!" The dinner guests were amazed at this daring thought, and one said that if Davitt went there when fury and bitterness were so tense, he might be killed by a government supporter. Annie George replied, "How could Michael Davitt die better than with his people?" Her husband said little except that she had expressed his own feeling. But he repeated those words to her fifteen years later when his own life-or-death decision had to be made.

Late in 1883 George sailed to the British Isles for a second speaking tour. The highlight of this trip was a section of a speech in London that caused a storm of controversy to erupt around him. He spoke to an overflow audience in St. James's Hall. Every seat was taken and every foot of available standing room was filled. Even the platform was crowded with listeners. George spoke of the poor of London who needed justice rather than charity. Justice required that the land should be returned to the people without cost. But if doing this would work a hardship on some, like the helpless widows, provision could be made for them. The case of the widow was constantly being brought forward. Statistics showed some 200,000 widows in England of all kinds and ages. Every widow, cried George, from the lady who sat on the throne down to the poorest laborer's widow, could receive, not as a matter of charity but as a matter of justice, a pension of £100 a year. Laughter, cheers and some hissing followed this. The Tory papers the next day denounced George for disrespect to the Queen. George wrote to his wife, "I can't begin to send you the papers in which I am discussed, attacked and commented on, for I would have to send all the English, Scottish and Irish press. I am getting advertised to my heart's content, and I shall have crowds wherever I go."

During George's third trip to the United Kingdom in 1884-85, Helen Taylor wrote to Annie George: "Mr. George's name is in our papers every day for praise or blame, and he has more warm friends here than bitter enemies." British friends urged him to stand for Parliament, assuring him that he could be elected in any one of a number of constituencies. He replied that the accident of birth in the United States would place him at a disadvantage in an election campaign in England. He did not deem such a step prudent "unless there was such a considerable call as made it seem clearly my duty." There the matter was dropped.

In addition to speaking tours in the United Kingdom and Canada, George was invited to go to Australia. This he did with his wife in 1890, and it was his last trip abroad. This was to be their honeymoon, he said. He had sailed to Melbourne at fifteen as a member of the crew. Annie George was born in Sidney, Australia. On their arrival there in 1890, she was presented with a red and gold shoulder ribbon with "Welcome, Australia's Daughter" marked on it in large letters. George complimented his hosts on some states in his own country adopting the Australian or secret ballot. Before that each party published lists of its candidates that supporters asked for and deposited in the ballot boxes. George asked for more return traffic from Australia to the United States in the ideas of democracy. In the three months that George spent on this lecture tour, he spoke almost every day, and sometimes twice a day.

Altogether, between 1881 and 1890, George visited and lectured in the United Kingdom six times, the last time being on his return trip from Australia.

George's Fight Against Poverty—His Own and the World's

In 1880, a year after *Progress and Poverty* was published, George moved to New York City. He arrived there almost penniless and with debts in California still unpaid; he lived in New York for the rest of his life. George probably was the only author whose books sold by the million in his own lifetime without yielding him so much as a decent living. In December, 1880, he wrote to a friend that "I am afloat at 42, poorer than at 21. I do not complain; but there is some bitterness in it."

In the night of October 12, 1883, George wrote a note to his wife, and left it for her to find the next morning:

It is twenty-three years ago to-night since we first met—I only a month or two older than Harry, and you not much older than our Jen. For twenty-three years we have been closer to each other than to any one else in the world, and I think we esteem each other more and love each other better than when we first began to love. You are now "fat, fair and forty," and to me the mature woman is handsomer and more lovable than the slip of a girl whom twenty-three years ago I met without knowing that my life was to be bound up with hers. We are not rich—so poor just now, in fact, that all I can give you on this anniversary is a little love letter; but there is no one we can afford to envy, and in each other's love we have what no wealth could compensate for. And so let us go on, true and loving, trusting in Him to carry us further who has brought us so far with so little to regret. For twenty-three years you have been mine and I have been yours, and though twenty-three years your husband, I am more than ever your lover.[1]

Shortly before this date he wrote to a friend, "I have now just $25 in the world, about half a week's living with economy; no, not that. However, this is no new experience to me."

Tom L. Johnson and others gave George financial support in his later years, so that he didn't have to lecture and write magazine articles to

---

1. Henry George, Jr., *The Life of Henry George* (New York: Robert Schalkenbach Foundation, 1960), pp. 412-413. [Originally published in 1900.]

earn a living. Johnson also contributed $80,000 during 1895-96 to the *Recorder* of Cleveland, a paper that supported the single tax idea. In the last year of his life George and his family occupied the only home they ever owned, in Fort Hamilton, New York. Johnson gave them the land, and a legacy from England enabled them to pay for the house.

George was always sensitive to the poverty around him. In the speech George delivered in Glasgow on February 18, 1884 (quoted in Chapter 4), he reiterated his concern about poverty, as he always did:

[I]t is from Glasgow men some of my blood, at least, is drawn. I am not proud of it. If I were a Glasgow man to-day I would not be proud of it. Here you have a great and rich city, and here you have poverty and destitution that would appal a heathen. Right on these streets of yours the very stranger can see sights that he could not see in any tribe of savages in anything like normal conditions. "Let Glasgow Flourish by the Preaching of the Word"—that is the motto of this great, proud city. What sort of a Word is it that here has been preached? Or, let your preaching have been what it may, what is your practice? Are these the fruits of the Word—this poverty, this destitution, this vice and degradation? To call this a Christian community is a slander on Christianity. Low wages, want, vice, degradation—these are not the fruits of Christianity. They come from the ignoring and denial of the vital principles of Christianity. Yet you people in Glasgow not merely erect church after church, you have the cheek to subscribe money to send missionaries to the heathen. I wish the heathen were a little richer, that they might subscribe money and send missionaries to such so-called Christian communities as this—to point to the luxury, the very ostentation of wealth, on the one hand, and to the bare-footed, ill-clad women on the other; to your men and women with bodies stunted and minds distorted; to your little children growing up in such conditions that only a miracle can keep them pure!

George described certain parts of Ireland he had seen where the land was good but the human population was sparse. Sheep and cattle had displaced people, and traces of ruined hamlets could be found, for raising livestock was more profitable than tilling the soil. The owners of the land, many of whom lived in London and Paris, drove their tenants away. In the areas of bog and rock, however, in the mountains and at the seashore, the dense population struggled to make a living tilling the soil that was too poor for grazing.

George's description of Ireland can be applied to most of Latin

America today, where the ownership of land is distributed very unequally. The steep hillsides are suitable for grazing; the flat, fertile valley lands are best for tillage. The big landowners, having gained possession of the best valley lands, have found cattle-ranching more profitable than tillage. Consequently the poor peasants have been pushed to the hillsides, where they scratch out a living on steep slopes that are overcrowded and eroding badly. World Bank experts, in a number of studies on Latin American countries, pointed out that the system of land use is wrong; cattle should be on the hillsides for limited grazing, and the tillers of the soil should be on the flat valley lands. What they did not point out was that it was not ignorance that perpetuated destructive land use, but the self-interest of the big land grabbers.[2] The problems Henry George dealt with are largely unsolved in most of the poor countries.

In addition to writing and lecturing, George's concern about poverty and his remedy for it led him to undertake two spectacular campaigns for mayor of New York City.

George's Two Campaigns for Mayor of New York City

The unions of New York City entered politics in the fall of 1886, and they invited George to be their candidate for mayor. He was eager to promote his views in a political campaign, but he was afraid of a crushing defeat that would do more harm than good. He therefore laid down a condition before accepting the nomination: at least 30,000 voters should sign a pledge to support and vote for him. The unions met this requirement, gathering over 34,000 signatures, for the workers' response to George was enthusiastic. The Democratic politicans were shaken as signatures rolled in from what had been their strongholds.

An incident occurred early in this campaign which was not revealed by George until a few days before his death eleven years later. The Democratic Party sent an emissary to meet privately and secretly with George in a Manhattan restaurant. George was told that he couldn't possibly be elected mayor no matter how many people voted for him. But if he refused the nomination for mayor, Tammany Hall and the

---

2. See Jacob Oser, *Promoting Economic Development, with Illustrations from Kenya* (Evanston: Northwestern University Press, 1967), pp. 103-105.

County Democrats would nominate him for a seat in the House of Representatives in Washington. A safe district would be selected, and he would be guaranteed election. There would be no campaign, no expense to George, and he could leave for Europe or anywhere else he wanted to go; when he returned he would receive a certificate of election. George finally asked:

"You tell me I cannot possibly get the office. Why, if I cannot possibly get the office, do you want me to withdraw?" His reply was: "You cannot be elected, but your running will raise hell!" I said: "You have relieved me of embarrassment. I do not want the responsibility and the work of the office of the Mayor of New York, but I do want to raise hell! I am decided and will run."[3]

Delegates from nearly every union in the city, representing 40,900 workingmen, met on September 23, 1886, and nominated Henry George. The *New York Times* reported that "the delegates rose in a body and cheered. Hats, handkerchiefs, and canes were flung in the air, men stamped on the floor until the building shook, and for a time the noise was deafening."

The nominating convention adopted a platform written by George; parts of it read as follows:

IV. We declare the crowding of so many of our people into narrow tenements at enormous rents while half the area of the city is yet unbuilt upon to be a scandalous evil, and that to remedy this state of things all taxes on buildings and improvements should be abolished, so that no fine shall be put upon the employment of labor in increasing living accommodations, and that taxes should be levied on land irrespective of improvements, so that those who are now holding land vacant shall be compelled either to build on it themselves or to give up the land to those who will.

V. We declare furthermore that the enormous value which the presence of a million and a half of people gives to the land of this city belongs properly to the whole community; that it should not go to the enrichment of individuals and corporations, but should be taken in taxation and applied to the improvement and beautifying of the city, to the promotion of the health, comfort, education, and recreation of its people, and to the providing of means of transit commensurate with the needs of a great metropolis. We also declare that the existing means of

3. Henry George, Jr., *The Life of Henry George*, p. 463.

transit should not be left in the hands of corporations, which, while gaining enormous profits from the growth of population, oppress their employees and provoke strikes that interrupt travel and imperil the public peace, but should by lawful process be assumed by the city and operated for public benefit.[4]

The campaign was financed by collections at George's meetings and by some of his close friends, principally Tom L. Johnson. All the daily newspapers of New York City opposed George except a small German-language socialist paper. A new daily paper, *The Leader,* was created during the campaign to support George. Its circulation jumped to 35,000 almost immediately. To make the paper self-supporting, all the work of editors and reporters was contributed without pay. Though the other newspapers all opposed George, their sub-editors and reporters almost unanimously supported him. Many of them worked two shifts each day, one on their regular jobs, and one as unpaid volunteers on *The Leader.*

George campaigned tirelessly, sometimes speaking as frequently as twelve or fourteen times a day. But the difficulties of his third-party movement were insuperable, for the law worked for the benefit of the party machines. There were no representatives of George in the polling places to count the votes. Under the election law each party had to print its own ballots and distribute them to voters to deposit in the ballot boxes; some of the election districts were actually without distributors and ballots.

The Democratic candidate, Abram S. Hewitt, once admired *Progress and Poverty* and when he was in Congress employed George to work on a Congressional report on labor; he won the election with 90,552 votes. George came in second with 68,110. The Republican candidate, Theodore Roosevelt, was third with 60,435 votes. It was widely believed that George had really won the election but was "counted out" at the end.

In 1897 George was again asked to run for mayor. New York had just been enlarged by the absorption of Brooklyn and other adjoining municipalities, and it was now the second city in the world in population. His physician had warned him against the ordeal that such a campaign would entail, especially because he had suffered a stroke

---

4. *The New York Times,* September 24, 1886, p. 2.

seven years earlier. One afternoon George asked another doctor, a neighbor and good friend of his, what the worst might be if he undertook another strenuous campaign. The doctor replied that it would most probably prove fatal. "But I have got to die," said George. "How can I die better than serving humanity? Besides, so dying will do more for the cause than anything I am likely to be able to do in the rest of my life."

Some close friends came to Mrs. George to emphasize the danger and advise her to influence her husband against campaigning. She answered:

> When I was a much younger woman I made up my mind to do all in my power to help my husband in his work, and now after many years I may say that I have never once crossed him in what he has seen clearly to be his duty. Should he decide to enter this campaign I shall do nothing to prevent him; but shall, on the contrary, do all I can to strengthen and encourage him. He must live his life in his own way and at whatever sacrifice his sense of duty requires; and I shall give him all I can—devotion.[5]

George called a meeting of his more intimate friends, and thirty people came to advise him on whether to enter the campaign. He listened to all the suggestions, but he cut short every reference to his health and strength. The only question, he said, was one of duty. As a result of this conference, he decided to make the fight.

When he reached home, Mr. George told his wife of the conference with the friends and then said:

"Annie: Remember what you declared Michael Davitt should do at the time of the Phoenix Park murders in 1882—go to Dublin and be with his people, even though it should cost him his life. I told you then that I might some day ask you to remember those words. I ask you now. Will you fail to tell me to go into this campaign? The people want me; they say they have no one else upon whom they can unite. It is more than a question of good government. If I enter the field it will be a question of natural rights, even though as mayor I might not directly be able to do a great deal for natural rights. New York will become the theatre of the world and my success will plunge our cause into world politics."

Mrs. George answered: "You should do your duty at whatever cost." And so it was decided that he should run.[6]

5. Henry George, Jr., *The Life of Henry George*, p. 595.
6. *Ibid.*, p. 597.

On October 5, 1897, Henry George was nominated for Mayor of Greater New York by the representatives of four Democratic factions united as The Democracy of Thomas Jefferson. An overflow meeting was held at Cooper Union, with every seat occupied and men and women filling the aisles and standing twenty deep around the walls. Outside the hall 8,000 people who could not get in met in support of George. The *New York Times* commented on the frenzied response from the crowd when George appeared at the meeting, and it described the scene when he completed his acceptance speech:

> Mr. George does not appear in robust health. He seemed exhausted when he had finished speaking. Mrs. George ran to him and wiped his brow with her handkerchief and ex-Congressman Johnson helped him on with his overcoat, and with his arm around him forced a passage for him from the platform, where a crowd thronged around demanding to shake hands with him.[7]

Tom L. Johnson was George's campaign manager. The platform announced at the Cooper Union meeting hailed William Jennings Bryan, presidential candidate on the Democratic ticket the year before. The platform called for municipal ownership of franchises; for lower gas and street car fares; for the extension of parks, libraries, museums and free schools; for wise, equitable and scientific taxation; and against rule by injunction that infringes on the people's right to assemble peacefully, to march in the streets and to speak freely.

Although there was nothing in the platform on the single tax, George said he would run as a single taxer, as an absolute free trader, as an opponent of liquor taxes and as a greenbacker, favoring paper money as against the gold standard.

The campaign aroused great interest in the United Kingdom, where George was well known as the result of his six lecture tours there and the wide circulation of his books. The *New York Times* reported the following reactions from two London newspapers:

> LONDON, Oct. 4—The newspapers here generally pay much attention to the New York political campaign, publishing long articles, dispatches, and editorials on the subject.

---

7. *The New York Times,* October 6, 1897, p. 2.

The Globe says:

"Judging from the Times's dispatch, Henry George will be the next Mayor. The Americans do not exceed a quarter of the whole population, and the European Anarchists, Socialists, Italians, Poles, Hungarians, and Russians, all the very lowest of their race, will support the man whose childish economics and wild theories are derided in every capital in Europe."[8]

THE LONDON TIMES ON GEORGE

It Says that to Win He Must Be Supported by Dangerous Classes

LONDON, Oct. 6.—The Times, commenting editorially this morning on the "increasing seriousness of Henry George's candidature for the Mayoralty of Greater New York," says:

"It is humiliating to think that there is any possibility of his being the first Mayor of the enlarged New York. No doubt in past times there have been worse candidates. Mr. George is honest, but he is the nominee of the Silverites, and, what is worse, can only be returned by his winning the support of the dangerous classes, who will afterward demand their price for their services."[9]

From October 16 to 28 George made thirty speeches, and on five of those days, including the day he died, he spoke four times. His last speech on October 28, the Thursday before election day, was at the Manhattan Opera House. He arrived there after most of the crowd had left, and he rambled on in a way that distressed the audience that remained. Mrs. George, who always accompanied him, got him back to the Union Square Hotel at midnight. "I am very tired," said George as his friends crowded around him. He had a light meal and went to bed, attributing his discomfort to indigestion. At 2:30 A.M. Mrs. George heard her husband walking about the room. "I don't feel well," he said, "but I suppose it does not amount to much." She urged him to go back to bed, but he continued to sit in an arm chair. She called her son, Henry George, Jr., from an adjoining room; together they helped the sick man back to bed, and they called his doctor, who arrived at 4:00 A.M. Within an hour George was dead of a stroke at 58 years of age.

Of the many obituaries, two will be cited here from the closest friends of George.

---

8. *The New York Times,* October 5, 1897, p. 3.
9. *The New York Times,* October 6, 1897, p. 2.

Tom L. Johnson wrote:

That first meeting with Mr. George was the beginning of a friendship which grew stronger with each passing day and which, it seemed to me, had reached the full flower of perfection when I stood at his bedside in the Union Square Hotel in New York City the night of October 28, 1897, and saw his tired eyes close in their last sleep.[10]

The other tribute came from the Reverend Doctor Edward McGlynn, a native New Yorker, once pastor of St. Stephen's Catholic Church, one of the largest in New York City. He was a disciple of George and an activist in the single tax movement. For this he was excommunicated in 1887, but he was reinstated in the Church in 1892, perhaps partly because of George's open letter to Pope Leo XIII the year before. He was summoned to the hotel where George had died. Only a few days earlier, in speaking of his friendship for Dr. McGlynn, George had said, "I would rather have Dr. McGlynn at my dying bedside than any man I know." Dr. McGlynn was greatly grieved at his friend's death, saying, "He died in a struggle for human liberty. His spirit will live in the hearts of his friends. He died like a hero on the field of battle."

There was a great outpouring of grief at the death of Henry George. Two Episcopal ministers and Dr. McGlynn conducted the funeral service. He was buried on Monday, November 1, 1897, in Greenwood Cemetery, Brooklyn, beside his daughter Jennie, who had died six months earlier.

The supporters of Henry George nominated his son, Henry George, Jr., to fill the vacant spot in the race for mayor of New York City. The election, held the day after George's funeral, saw Robert A. Van Wyck win with 228,531 votes; he was the candidate of the Tammany Hall faction of the Democratic Party. Seth Low, representing the Democrats opposed to Tammany and the Citizens' Union, ran second with 148,215 votes. Benjamin F. Tracy, Republican, received 101,994 votes. Henry George, Jr., had 19,836 votes.

Henry George's ideas lived on after his death. In the ebb and flow of political and social movements, the single tax idea has suffered a decline in recent decades. But the movement continues, kept alive by disciples of George.

10. Tom L. Johnson, *My Story* (London: J. M. Dent & Sons, Ltd., 1913), p. 52.

Selected Bibliography

A rich source of material by and about Henry George is published by the Robert Schalkenbach Foundation, 50 East 69 Street, New York, 10021. Robert Schalkenbach (1856-1924), a wealthy printer, was an honorary pallbearer at the funeral of George. When he died, he left most of his estate in a trust fund for the education of the public in the economic principles developed by George. The Robert Schalkenbach Foundation was incorporated in 1925 to administer this fund. The first eight books listed below are kept in print and sold at moderate prices by this foundation.

Henry George's first and most famous book was *Progress and Poverty,* originally published in 1879. Its subtitle is: *An Inquiry into the Cause of Industrial Depressions and of Increase of Want with Increase of Wealth. . . The Remedy.*

Another work by George is *The Land Question.* This volume contains three separate books. The first is "The Land Question," first published in 1881 under the title of *The Irish Land Question.* In order better to indicate the general character of this topic, and to conform to the title under which it had been republished in other countries, the title was subsequently changed to *The Land Question.* In this book George considered the distressed conditions of Ireland struggling under the yoke of English landlordism. He argued that a change of government would not help much if the system of land ownership were not changed also.

The second book contained in *The Land Question* is called "Property in Land. A Passage-at-Arms between the Duke of Argyll and Henry George." The Duke's attack on George is printed here; it appeared as an article called "The Prophet of San Francisco" in the journal *Nineteenth Century* for April, 1884. George's reply first appeared in the same journal for July, 1884, under the title "The 'Reduction to Iniquity.' "

The third book included in *The Land Question* reprinted the English translation of the Encyclical Letter of Pope Leo XIII on the Condition of Labor, issued in 1891. It also contains George's "The Condition of Labor. An Open Letter to Pope Leo XIII."

The third book on the Robert Schalkenbach Foundation list is George's *Social Problems.* The first thirteen chapters appeared originally in 1883 as articles in *Frank Leslie's Illustrated Newspaper,* which had contracted to carry the series. Even before all the articles had been published, George had antagonized enough people so that even *Frank Leslie's* published editorials criticizing him. George added eight chapters and a conclusion to the original thirteen chapters and published them all as a book in 1883.

In 1886 Henry George published *Protection or Free Trade. An Examination of the Tariff Question, with Especial Regard to the Interests of Labor.* He dedicated this book to the memory of the French Physiocrats of the last half of the eighteenth century, who advocated laissez faire, and especially free trade; this was in an era of extreme government intervention in economic affairs.

In 1892 George published *A Perplexed Philosopher. Being an Examination of Mr. Herbert Spencer's Various Utterances on the Land Question, with some Incidental Reference to His Synthetic Philosophy.* In 1850, twenty-nine years before *Progress and Poverty* appeared, Spencer had criticized the existing system of land tenure. George had given full credit to Spencer in *Progress and Poverty* for anticipating some of George's own ideas. How disappointing it was to George when Spencer in 1892 revised his earlier work and omitted all mention of the inequity of property in land. In *A Perplexed Philosopher,* George attacked what he considered to be Spencer's desertion of a noble cause.

George's last book was *The Science of Political Economy.* He hoped, in this book, to present a complete reconstruction of political economy in the light of his own views on the subject. He began writing it in 1891, but other projects prevented him from completing it. The book was published posthumously in 1898 exactly as he left it, except for minor editing.

In addition to these six books by Henry George, the Robert Schalkenbach Foundation publishes pamphlets containing his speeches, articles, and editorials. It also publishes pamphlets and books about George and the single-tax movement. One book is the outstanding biography, *The Life of Henry George,* written by his son, Henry George, Jr., and published in 1900. Another book is a collection of readings called *Land-Value Taxation Around the World. Reports on Current and Historical Efforts to Apply the Principle of Collecting the Community-Created Value of land for Community Benefit,* 1955. This book of readings has eight pages devoted to the single tax community of Fairhope, Alabama, founded in 1894. A more extensive treatment of this Georgeite community can be found in Paul E. and Blanche R. Alyea, *Fairhope, 1894-1954. The Story of a Single Tax Colony* (The University of Alabama Press, 1956).

The New York Public Library at 42nd Street and Fifth Avenue contains a vast treasury of Henry George literature. George's daughter, Anna George de Mille, gave a large collection to the library in 1925; it includes letters, scrapbooks, newspaper clippings, George's manuscripts, and other material. The library has at least nineteen different editions of *Progress and Poverty,* including abridged editions and translations in French, Spanish, and Chinese. One example of the fascinating material on George in this library is his speech, "Scotland and Scotsmen," delivered in Glasgow on February 18, 1884. Unfortunately this scintillating lecture is no longer reprinted, but it has been quoted above on pages 78 and 113.

Among the newspapers and magazines, important material on George and the taxation of land can be found in the back issues of *The American Journal of Economics and Sociology;* this quarterly journal was founded in 1941 by the Robert Schalkenbach Foundation. *The New York Times* has a vast number of news stories, editorials, and articles on George. *Land and Freedom,* formerly *The Single Tax Review,* had many informative editorials, articles, letters from readers, reports from special correspondents abroad, speeches, activities of single tax clubs, reviews of single tax literature, and proceedings of various Henry George congresses. It was published in New York City as a quarterly during 1901-7, and as a bimonthly during 1908-43, when it ceased publication.

Below is a list of additional works on Henry George and his ideas.

BARKER, CHARLES ALBRO. *Henry George.* New York:
Oxford University Press, 1955.

BIRNIE, ARTHUR. *Single-Tax George.* London: Thomas Nelson and Sons Ltd., 1939.

BRAMWELL, LORD. *Nationalisation of Land, a Review of Mr. Henry George's "Progress and Poverty,"* 5th ed. London: Liberty & Property Defence League, 1885.

CORD, STEVEN B. *Henry George: Dreamer or Realist?* Philadelphia: University of Pennsylvania Press, 1965.

DE MILLE, ANNA GEORGE. *Henry George, Citizen of the World.* Chapel Hill: The University of North Carolina Press, 1950.

GEIGER, GEORGE R. *The Philosophy of Henry George.* New York: The Macmillan Company, 1933.

JOHNSON, TOM L. *My Story.* London: J. M. Dent & Sons, Ltd., 1913.

LAWRENCE, ELWOOD P. *Henry George in the British Isles.* East Lansing: The Michigan State University Press, 1957.

LONGE, FRANCIS D. *A Critical Examination of Mr. George's "Progress and Poverty" and Mr. Mill's Theory of Wages.* London: Simpkin & Marshall, 1883.

LEWIS, ARTHUR M. *Ten Blind Leaders of the Blind.* Chicago: Charles H. Kerr & Company, 1910.

NOCK, ALBERT JAY. *Henry George.* New York: William Morrow & Company, 1939.

POST, LOUIS F. *Taxation of Land Values,* 5th ed. Indianapolis: The Bobbs-Merrill Company, 1915.

POST, LOUIS F. *The Prophet of San Francisco.* New York: The Vanguard Press, 1930.

RAE, JOHN. *Contemporary Socialism,* 2nd ed. New York: Charles Scribner's Sons, 1891.

ROSE, EDWARD J. *Henry George.* New York: Twayne Publishers, 1968.

SANBORN, F. B. (ed.) *The Single Tax Discussion Held at Saratoga September 5, 1890.* Reported for the American Social Science Association. Concord, Mass.: 1890.

TOYNBEE, ARNOLD. *"Progress and Poverty," a Criticism*

of Mr. Henry George. Being Two Lectures Delivered in St. Andrew's Hall, Newman Street, London. London: Kegan Paul, Trench & Company, 1883.

YOUNG, ARTHUR. *Single Tax Movement in the United States.* Princeton: Princeton University Press, 1915.

Index

Alta California, 12, 24
Alyca, Blanche R., 123
Alyea, Paul E., 123
American Economic Association, 79
The American Journal of Economics
    and Sociology, 123
Appleton, George S., 17
Argyll, Duke of, 121
Associated Press, 12, 26

Bible, 17, 48, 68
Blanc, Louis, 74
Boer War, 109
British Times and Mirror, 76
Browning, Elizabeth Barrett, 40-41
Bryan, William Jennings, 14, 82, 118

California, University of, 29-31
California Home Journal, 11, 22
Capitalism, 83-84
Catholic social movement, 97
Catholic trade unions, 97
Central Pacific Railroad Company, 26
China, 93-94
Civil War of the United States, 20, 24,
    89
Cleveland Recorder, 113
Columbia College, 79
Communists, 68, 83-84
Comparative advantage, law of, 96
Compensation to landowners, 46-47,
    81, 87, 98
The Condition of the Working Class
    in England, 83-84
Congressional Record, 71
Cooperatives, 45, 76, 97, 100

Daniel (of the Bible), 78
D. Appleton and Company, 32
Davitt, Michael, 109-110, 117
De Leon, Daniel, 83
Democratic Party, 12-14, 20, 28,
    114-115, 118, 120
Dewey, John, 69

Diminishing returns, law of, 36-38,
    56-62, 105-107
Dove, Patrick Edward, 105
Du Pont Corporation, 65

Egypt, 48, 96
Encyclical Letter on the Condition of
    Labor, 96-101, 122
Engels, Friedrich, 83-84
Eton College, 108

Fairhope, 1894-1954. The Story of a
    Single Tax Colony, 123
Farm product prices in the United
    States, 37
Farms, size of, 42, 64, 87-88
Favorable balance of trade, 95-96
Feudalism, 83
Florida price of land, 54
Fourier, Charles, 74
Frank Leslie's Illustrated Newspaper,
    88, 122
Free trade, 71

Garland, Hamlin, 82
Garrison, William Lloyd, 75
Garrison, William LLoyd (the young-
    er), 82
General Motors Corporation, 65
George, Anna Angela, 13, 31, 69, 123
George, Annie Fox, 11, 22-23, 27,
    109-111, 117-119
George, Catherine, 11, 17, 29
George, Henry
    on Alta California, 12, 24
    arrested in Ireland, 13, 108-109
    in Australia, 11, 14, 17, 19, 69,
    111
    on California Home Journal, 11,
    22
    campaigns for mayor of New
    York City, 13-14, 69, 81,
    114-119

in Canada, 11, 13, 17, 21, 69, 111
childhood, 11, 17-18
on Chinese question, 12, 26
on compensation to landowners, 46-47, 81, 87
on cooperatives, 45
death, 14, 69, 119-120
and the Democratic Party, 12-14, 20, 28, 114-115, 118
on diminishing returns, 36-38, 105-107
on favorable balance of trade, 95-96
in France, 13
on "fresh-air funds," 90
on government regulation, 45, 50, 66
on harmony of interests, 41, 48-50, 101-102
on infant industries, 94-95
on interest, 39-41, 43, 49, 66
on land prices, 28, 40, 42-43, 52
on land speculation, 42-43
lectures, 13-14, 17-18, 28-29, 69, 78-80, 108-114
marriage, 11
on monopolies, 12, 26, 40, 43-44, 49, 55, 59, 66, 73, 80, 84, 88
on Oakland *Daily Transcript,* 12, 27
in poverty (his own), 21-23, 31, 112
on poverty, 29-31, 37-38, 40-45, 78, 86-87, 89-90, 94, 96, 113-114
on profit, 39, 47-48
on rent, 36-37, 39-43, 45-49, 51-53, 66, 82, 84, 86-87
on *Sacramento Reporter,* 12
on Sacramento *Union,* 11
on San Francisco *Chronicle,* 12, 25
on San Francisco *Daily Evening Journal,* 11
on San Francisco *Daily Evening Post,* 12, 19
on San Francisco *Evening Journal,* 11
on San Francisco *Herald,* 12, 26

on San Francisco *Times,* 12, 25
in school, 17-18
at sea, 11, 19-21
on seamen's rights, 19
on slavery, 20, 29, 74-75, 78, 101
on *The Standard,* 13-14
on tariffs, 92-96
on taxation, 45-50, 52-53, 62-63, 65, 72, 80, 87, 94, 96, 101, 104
typesetter, 11, 19, 21-25
on unemployment, 41-43, 45, 89, 91-92
union member, 11, 22, 71
on unions, 44-45, 66
in United Kingdom, 13-14, 17, 69, 78, 86-87, 108-113
on wages, 33-35, 38-41, 43-45, 47, 49, 51, 54-55, 64-67
on wages-fund theory, 33, 35, 51
on war, 37, 89
on women's rights, 27
George, Henry, writings of
"The Irish Land Question," 13, 86-87, 121
"The Land Question," 13, 86-87, 121
"An Open Letter to Pope Leo XIII," 14, 96-102, 122
"Our Land and Land Policy, National and State," 12, 28, 104
A Perplexed Philosopher, 14, 73-75, 86, 122
"A Plea for the Supernatural," 24
Progress and Poverty, 12-13, 17, 25, 27, 31-70, 73, 76, 81-82, 85-86, 103-105, 108-109, 116, 121-123
"Property in Land. A Passage-at-Arms between the Duke of Argyll and Henry George," 121
Protection or Free Trade, 13, 70-71, 92-96, 122
"The Reduction to Iniquity," 121
The Science of Political Economy, 14, 103-107, 122
"Scotland and Scotsmen," 78, 113, 123
"Sic Semper Tyrannis!," 12, 24

Social Problems, 13, 70, 72-73, 88-92, 122
"What the Railroad will Bring Us," 12, 25-26
George, Jr., Henry, 11, 23, 103, 119-120, 123
George, Jennie Teresa, 12, 25, 120
George, Richard, 11, 17
George, Richard Fox, 11, 23
Goldman, Eric F., 70
Government regulation, 45, 50, 66-68, 73, 76, 84-85, 99-100, 122
Greeley, Horace, 12, 26, 28

Hamilton, Alexander, 95
Harmony of interests, 41, 48-50, 65, 77, 98-102
Harper (publisher), 32
Harte, Bret, 25
Hayes, Rutherford B., 29
Haymarket affair, 83
Hewitt, Abram S., 116
Hindoo, 11, 19
Hobson, John A., 69
Homestead Act, 65
House of Representatives, 71

Increasing returns to scale, 56, 61-62
Infant industry argument, 94-95
Initiative, 71
Interest, 39-41, 43, 49, 52, 55, 66-67, 77-78
International Business Machines Corporation, 65
Ireland, 13, 86-87, 108-110, 121
Irish World, 108
Isaiah, 48

Jefferson, Thomas, 74, 118
Jesus Christ, 90, 99
Johnson, Tom L., 70, 92, 112-113, 116, 118, 120

King's College, Scotland, 105
Knights of Labor, 13, 71

Ladies' Land League of Ireland, 109-110
Land and Freedom, 123
Land League of Ireland, 109

Land prices, 28, 40, 42-43, 52-55, 62, 68, 79
Land speculation, 42-43, 53, 55
Land-Value Taxation Around the World, 123
Latin American land tenure, 113-114
Leo XIII, Pope, 14, 96-102, 120, 122
Lincoln, Abraham, 24-25
London *Globe,* 119
London *Times,* 119
Louis XV, King, 104
Low, Seth, 120

Malthus, Thomas Robert, 35-36, 38, 46, 56, 105
The Man with Forty Crowns, 67
Markham, Edwin, 82
Marshall, Alfred, 76-78
Marx, Karl, 55, 76, 83-84, 97
Massachusetts Institute of Technology, 79
McCloskey, Matthew, 22
McGlynn, Edward, 120
Mill, John Stuart, 12, 26-27, 30, 33, 40, 51, 108
de Mille, Agnes, 31
de Mille, Anna George, 69, 123
Monopolies, 12, 26, 40, 43-44, 49, 55, 59, 66, 70, 73, 76, 78, 80, 84-85, 88

New York *Herald,* 26
New York *Leader,* 116
New York price of land, 53-54
New York *Sun,* 88
The New York Times, 80-82, 115, 118-119, 123
New York Tribune, 12, 26
Nineteenth Century, 121
Nock, Albert Jay, 72

Oakland *Daily Transcript,* 12, 27
Ogilvie, William, 105
The Overland Monthly, 12, 25
Owen, Robert, 74

Parnell, Charles, 108
Pennsylvania Railroad, 54
Pensions, 78
Philosophical Society of Newcastle, 104

Phoenix Park murders, 110, 117
Physiocrats, 104, 122
Plato, 69
Post, Louis F., 82
Poverty, 29-31, 37-38, 40-45, 76-78, 81-84, 86-87, 89-90, 94, 96-100, 108-109, 113-115
Profit, 39, 47-48, 52, 66, 68

Quesnay, François, 104

Railroads, 12, 25-26, 31, 54
Recall, 71
Referendum, 71
Rent, 36-37, 39-43, 45-49, 51-53, 55, 58-59, 62, 66, 68, 76, 79, 84, 86-87
Rerum Novarum, 96-101, 122
Ricardo, David, 39, 51-52, 96
Robert Schalkenbach Foundation, 68, 121-123
Roosevelt, Theodore, 13, 116
Rousseau, Jean Jacques, 74

Sacramento Reporter, 12
Sacramento *Union*, 11
San Francisco *Chronicle*, 12, 25
San Francisco *Daily Evening Journal*, 11, 22
San Francisco *Daily Evening Post*, 12, 19, 28
San Francisco *Evening Journal*, 11
San Francisco *Herald*, 12, 26
San Francisco *Times*, 12, 25
Schalkenbach, Robert, 121
Scotland, 78, 113, 123
Scribner's, 32
Seabury, Samuel R., 82
Seligman, Edwin R. A., 79-80
Seton, Ernest Thompson, 82
Shaw, George Bernard, 84-85
Shubrick, 11, 20-21
The Single Tax Review, 123
Slavery, 20, 29, 74-75, 78, 83, 101
Smith, Adam, 33, 54, 65, 105

Socialists and socialism, 68, 80, 82-84, 101-102, 119
Social Statics, 73-75
Spence, Thomas, 104-105
Spencer, Herbert, 73-75, 105, 122
The Standard, 13-14
Steffens, Lincoln, 82
Sunrise, 19
Sun Yat-sen, 69

Tammany Hall, 114-115, 120
Tarbell, Ida M., 82
Tariffs, 71, 92-96
Taxation, 45-50, 52-53, 62-63, 65, 67-69, 72, 76-77, 79-80, 87, 94, 96, 101, 104-105, 115, 118
Taylor, Helen, 108, 111
Tilden, Samuel J., 12, 29
Tokyo price of land, 54
Tolstoy, Count Leo, 69
Toynbee, Arnold, 75-76
Tracy, Benjamin F., 120
Twain, Mark, 25

Unemployment, 41-43, 45, 67, 89, 91-92
Unions, 13, 44-45, 66, 76, 97, 100-101, 114-115
United States Bureau of Statistics, 88
United States Census Bureau, 88

Van Wyck, Robert A., 120
Victoria, Queen, 111
Voltaire, 67, 75

Wages, 33-35, 38-41, 43-45, 47, 49, 51-52, 54-55, 63-67, 76-77
Wages-fund theory, 33, 51
Walker, Francis A., 78, 88
Wealth of Nations, 54, 105
Western Union Telegraph Company, 12, 26
Westminster, Duke of, 49
World Bank, 114

Yale University, 78-79